PEAK D
ILLUSTRATED
WALKS

Trevor Yorke

COUNTRYSIDE BOOKS
NEWBURY, BERKSHIRE

COUNTRYSIDE BOOKS
3 Catherine Road
Newbury, Berkshire

To view our complete range of books,
please visit us at
www.countrysidebooks.co.uk

ISBN 1 85306 854 3

Photographs and illustrations by the author

Produced through MRM Associates Ltd., Reading
Printed by Woolnough Bookbinding Ltd., Irthlingborough

CONTENTS

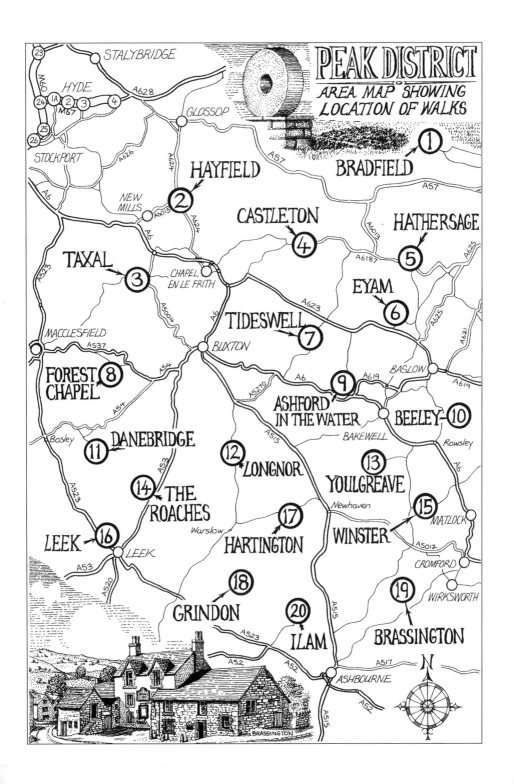

INTRODUCTION

From the vivid green hills broken upon their crests by outcrops of clawed white limestone, to the patchwork of earth colours formed by shimmering grass and wiry heather over the moors, the Peak District is a unique area of contrasts. There are deep gorges and caves, lofty hills and viewpoints, hidden river valleys and villages with rustic stone cottages and ancient pubs. Beneath this veneer of natural beauty is another dimension, the hand of man, from stone circles and burial mounds older than Stonehenge to the ruins of castles, mills and mines, melancholic sites which nature has reclaimed.

The problem though with walking in the Peak District where there is so much to see is that you would have to carry a library around in your rucksack just to understand the wide array of features you are likely to find. Unfortunately, many walking books are full of pages of monotonous text, guiding you around but not taking much time to explain what you see. However, in the *Illustrated Walks* books there are easy to follow maps showing you the way, leaving room for text and drawings to give extra information about the features you encounter on the route.

To ensure that you successfully negotiate the walks, the maps are divided into strips whereby you follow the route up or down the page in the direction of the arrows. This permits a larger scale and therefore allows me to show those small details on the ground that can make the difference between taking the correct route or not. With the addition of shading and contours I have given the maps a third dimension, so they are more like an aerial photograph than a confusing myriad of symbols!

The twenty circular walks in the book were carefully planned to offer a variety of landscapes. One can become unresponsive to even the most inspiring of settings after a while, so the routes pass through woodland, over moors, along streams and weave through back streets to add interest to the journey. There is a selection of distances, from those around 3 miles where time may be tight, to some over 5 miles for the more adventurous. Although some of the circuits may involve walking up hills, I have tried to choose paths with a gentle gradient, so even an inexperienced walker will hopefully find the longer routes manageable. Most importantly, there will be a pub or tearoom awaiting the weary traveller beside or close to the parking place.

All the routes use public footpaths, although there are a few concessionary paths where landowners have permitted access but can withdraw it, so alternative routes are shown for use if necessary. Since preparing the book, large areas of the Peaks have been opened up under the Rights of Way Act and it may be possible to further explore some of the places through which the walks pass. The latest Ordnance Survey Explorer maps, OL 1 and 24, mark those areas where you have a right to roam.

I hope that you will find the format of this book attractive and easy to follow, whether you are an enthusiastic rambler or simply an armchair walker! Just as importantly, I hope you get enjoyment from exploring new places and discovering more about your old favourites.

Trevor Yorke

USING THE BOOK

STEP 1: With the map of the Peak District shown on page 4 or a road atlas, find your way to the area. Then use the location map and the 'GETTING THERE' text to guide you to the parking place. *Please note these may be public car parks which have a charge or just spaces alongside a road where it is important not to block gates or driveways. Pub car parks are not used, although you could seek landlord's permission if you wish.*

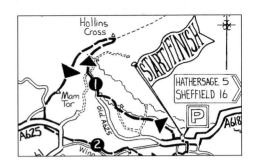

STEP 2: The walk begins at the START/FINISH flag on the first strip map, which will generally be a prominent point near to the parking place, and you should set off in the direction of the arrows. The 'START' text will help you get under way. *There are also snippets of text as you go, to guide you through trickier parts of the walk where the route may not be clear.*

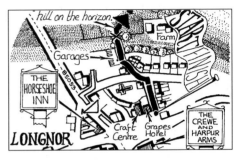

STEP 3: When you reach the number in a black circle, turn to the next strip map and continue from the corresponding number on that page. *The faint lines and shading are approximate contours (only judged by eye) to give you a feel for the landscape. The dark areas are high ground, the light are low.*

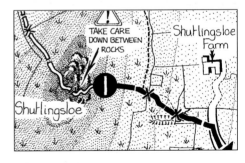

OTHER SYMBOLS

Rivers and Canals:

Small streams:

Main roads:

Other surfaced roads:

Tracks:

Paths:

Railways:

Hedges, Walls and Fences:

Rock outcrops:

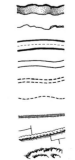

Parking place:

Buildings:

Churches:

Trees:

Woodland:

Rough grassland:

Embankments:

Cuttings and Pits:

Stiles or Gates:

Walk 1
BRADFIELD AND DALE DIKE
Length 5 miles

St. Nicholas's Church, High Bradfield

*I*t's hard to imagine that this quiet and colour-ful corner of South Yorkshire was the scene of the worst man-made disaster in British history. On the night of 11th March 1864 the newly constructed Dale Dike Dam burst, flooding the valley down to Sheffield with millions of gal-lons of water and taking the lives of nearly 250 people. There is nothing today to show that the heart of Bradfield Dale was ripped out on that cold winter's night; the physical scars have long healed, houses and the reservoir have been rebuilt and trees planted. Nowadays these fea-tures add variety to the landscape of stone walled fields and colourful moorland which blanket the hills while the gritstone villages of Low and High Bradfield make attractive destinations.

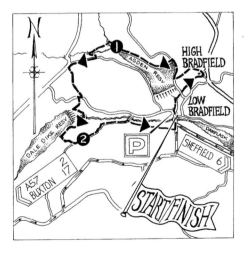

TERRAIN: Two steady climbs of about 300 ft. There is a mix of road walking and paths, some slippery.

GETTING THERE: Bradfield is 6 miles west of Sheffield. Approach by using the B6077 out of the city and then turn left onto the B6076 to Low Bradfield at Damflask. Fol-

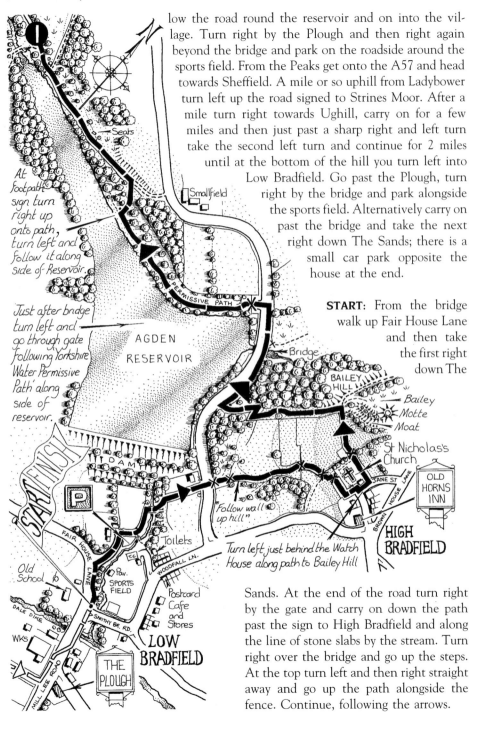

At footpath sign turn right up onto path, turn left and follow it along side of Reservoir.

Just after bridge turn left and go through gate following Yorkshire Water Permissive Path along side of reservoir.

low the road round the reservoir and on into the village. Turn right by the Plough and then right again beyond the bridge and park on the roadside around the sports field. From the Peaks get onto the A57 and head towards Sheffield. A mile or so uphill from Ladybower turn left up the road signed to Strines Moor. After a mile turn right towards Ughill, carry on for a few miles and then just past a sharp right and left turn take the second left turn and continue for 2 miles until at the bottom of the hill you turn left into Low Bradfield. Go past the Plough, turn right by the bridge and park alongside the sports field. Alternatively carry on past the bridge and take the next right down The Sands; there is a small car park opposite the house at the end.

START: From the bridge walk up Fair House Lane and then take the first right down The

Sands. At the end of the road turn right by the gate and carry on down the path past the sign to High Bradfield and along the line of stone slabs by the stream. Turn right over the bridge and go up the steps. At the top turn left and then right straight away and go up the path alongside the fence. Continue, following the arrows.

⊞**HIGH BRADFIELD:** As the name suggests this is the upper part of Bradfield and the more important historically, with the remains of two castles and the parish church. St Nicholas's is an outstandingly pure example of Perpendicular architecture, that is with the emphasis on soaring vertical lines (note the window bars and pinnacles), which was the vogue when this church was rebuilt in the 1480s. Inside, the original humble Norman edifice is still evident in the two round columns on the north arcade while just behind these are the remains of an even earlier Saxon cross which was found in a field at Low Bradfield in 1870. At the entrance to the church is the Watch House, built in 1831 to guard against grave robbers.

Smithy Bridge, Low Bradfield

⊞ **BAILEY HILL:** To the west of the church and just as you turn to go down the hill to Agden Reservoir there are the remains of a motte and bailey castle (probably 12th century) on your right. Although they are covered in trees you can still make out the moat (which was probably dry), the bank of the bailey above it and the motte on which the keep would have stood in the middle of the field behind it.

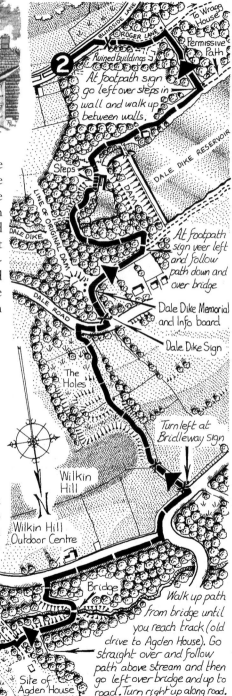

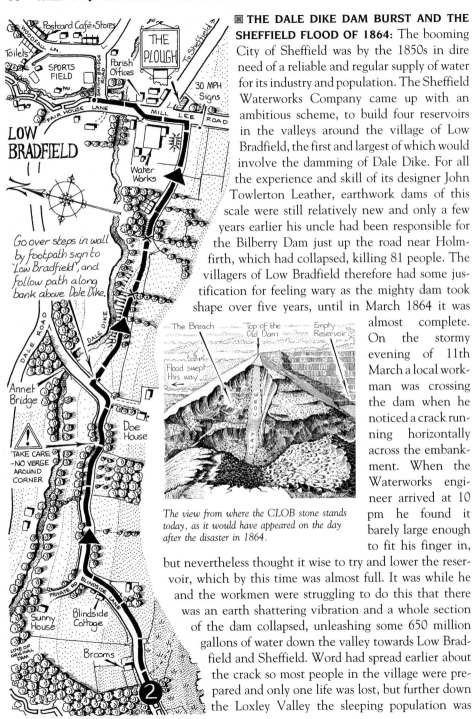

Postcard Café+Stores

WOODFALL

Toilets

SPORTS FIELD

PAV.

THE PLOUGH

Parish Offices

SMITHY BRIDGE ROAD

To Sheffield

30 MPH Signs

MILL LEE ROAD

FAIR HOUSE LANE

**LOW
BRADFIELD**

Water Works

Go over steps in wall by footpath sign to 'Low Bradfield', and follow path along bank above Dale Dike.

DALE ROAD

DALE DIKE

Annet Bridge

Doe House

⚠ TAKE CARE –NO VERGE AROUND CORNER

PRIVATE RD

BLINDSIDE LANE

Sunny House

Blindside Cottage

LINE OF ORIGINAL DAM

Brooms

2

▦ **THE DALE DIKE DAM BURST AND THE SHEFFIELD FLOOD OF 1864:** The booming City of Sheffield was by the 1850s in dire need of a reliable and regular supply of water for its industry and population. The Sheffield Waterworks Company came up with an ambitious scheme, to build four reservoirs in the valleys around the village of Low Bradfield, the first and largest of which would involve the damming of Dale Dike. For all the experience and skill of its designer John Towlerton Leather, earthwork dams of this scale were still relatively new and only a few years earlier his uncle had been responsible for the Bilberry Dam just up the road near Holmfirth, which had collapsed, killing 81 people. The villagers of Low Bradfield therefore had some justification for feeling wary as the mighty dam took shape over five years, until in March 1864 it was almost complete.

The Breach ···· Top of the ···· Empty ····
···· Old Dam ···· Reservoir ····

Flood swept this way ←

CLAY CORE

On the stormy evening of 11th March a local workman was crossing the dam when he noticed a crack running horizontally across the embankment. When the Waterworks engineer arrived at 10 pm he found it barely large enough to fit his finger in,

The view from where the CLOB stone stands today, as it would have appeared on the day after the disaster in 1864.

but nevertheless thought it wise to try and lower the reservoir, which by this time was almost full. It was while he and the workmen were struggling to do this that there was an earth shattering vibration and a whole section of the dam collapsed, unleashing some 650 million gallons of water down the valley towards Low Bradfield and Sheffield. Word had spread earlier about the crack so most people in the village were prepared and only one life was lost, but further down the Loxley Valley the sleeping population was

completely oblivious to the danger. Approximately 250 people, 400 houses, 100 factories, 20 bridges and more than 4,000 gardens were destroyed by what has become known as the Great Sheffield Flood, which is to this day the worst man-made disaster in British history. In the aftermath the city corporation, who were keen to take over the waterworks company, employed leading engineers to point the finger of blame at the design, in particular the pipes that ran beneath the dam. The company fought back, with its own panel of experts finding that a landslip adjacent to the structure was the reason for the collapse and it was hence an Act of God, which they had no responsibility for, an important factor as there was an ever increasing pile of compensation claims against them. When the commission sat to wade through these they made – to modern minds – some astonishing decisions on the levels of money to be awarded, for instance one man who had lost some furniture, a piano and some flowers was granted £110, yet one lady who had lost three children was only awarded £25 (people were assessed only on the loss of earning power). Worse still, the company had successfully gained permission from Parliament to increase water rates by 25% to avoid them going bankrupt, therefore, in effect, the poor people of Sheffield ended up paying for their own compensation! Despite the disaster, the dam building programme continued even though the exact cause of the collapse was still unknown. A new embankment a few hundred yards up the valley was com-

pleted in 1874 and still holds back the water of Dale Dike Reservoir.

⊞ **LOW BRADFIELD:** The whole strip of the village along Dale Dike was ripped out by the flood on that fateful night, although Smithy Bridge did survive. Today there is no sign of the devastation; trees line the river and cottages surround the cricket pitch, and the parish of Bradfield is still the largest in England.

REFRESHMENTS:

THE PLOUGH, New Road, Low Bradfield. Open weekdays 11.30 am to 3 pm and 5.30 pm to 11 pm (closed Monday lunchtime); Saturday 11.30 am to 11 pm; Sunday 12 noon to 10.30 pm. Telephone: 0114 285 1280.

THE OLD HORNS INN, High Bradfield. Open Monday, Tuesday and Thursday 12 noon to 4 pm and 5.30 pm to 11 pm; Wednesday, Friday and Saturday 11 am to 11 pm; Sunday 12 noon to 10.30 pm. Telephone: 0114 285 1207.

POSTCARD CAFE AND STORES, Woodfall Lane, Low Bradfield.

Walk 2
HAYFIELD
Length 3½ miles

View to Kinder Scout

Sometimes landscapes can unfold in front of your eyes like a theatre curtain, suddenly presenting the unsuspecting walker with a new awe-inspiring vista. This walk has such an impact. As you rise from the neatly boxed green slopes above the stone cottages of Hayfield a contrasting country unveils itself, with open moors cut into a patchwork of subtle colours, overshadowed by the dramatic rock face of Kinder Scout. The effect is repeated as you drop down towards Kinder Reservoir and the ridge of the plateau reflects in its tranquil waters. The return route passes through a wooded valley and along bubbling streams to the narrow lanes of Hayfield and a wide choice of ancient hostelries.

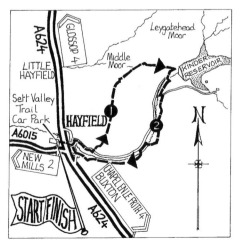

TERRAIN: One long but steady climb (500 ft approx). Some moorland paths can stay muddy all year. NB: Please keep to the designated paths, especially in spring when the grouse are nesting on the moors.

Hayfield

GETTING THERE: Hayfield is on the A624 halfway between Chapel en le Frith and Glossop. As you drop down into the village on the new bypass from either direction turn off onto the A6015 towards New Mills and the Sett Valley Trail car park. Take the first right just after the Kinder Scout Inn and then turn first left into the car park (pay and display).

START: From the car park head towards the village and cross the A624 at the pelican crossing. Go up past the church and turn left, over the bridge, and then as the road bends to the left cross over and walk up the path between the chemists and the little town lock up. At the top turn right and follow the lane for ¼ mile and then turn left by the old sign for the path to the Snake Inn, and follow it up into the hills.

⊠ **HAYFIELD:** This picturesque village clinging to the banks above the River Sett grew up around the textile industry. The old weavers' cottages with their distinctive long windows along the top floor (to allow the maximum light in for the workers) date from the

18th and early 19th century when Hayfield was booming. The River Sett has always been prone to flooding here; in 1748 bodies were swept from the graves and another flood 70 years later destroyed most of the medieval church. The edifice that replaced it, the present St Matthew's church, was raised up so that the columns of the old building are under the floor of the new. Just past Bank Street on the left is a memorial garden beside the falls, which are dedicated to three people who lost their lives in an accident at the 1983 Jazz Festival. Look out too for the terraced house festooned with all manner of gnomes and garden ornaments as you walk up the lane past the library.

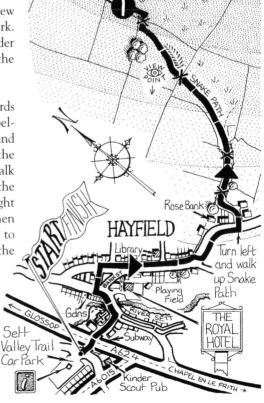

⊠ **MIDDLE MOOR:** The colourful patchwork patterns across this moorland are the result of skilful burning of the heather to create the ideal surroundings for grouse, new young shoots on which to feed and longer growth to hide in.

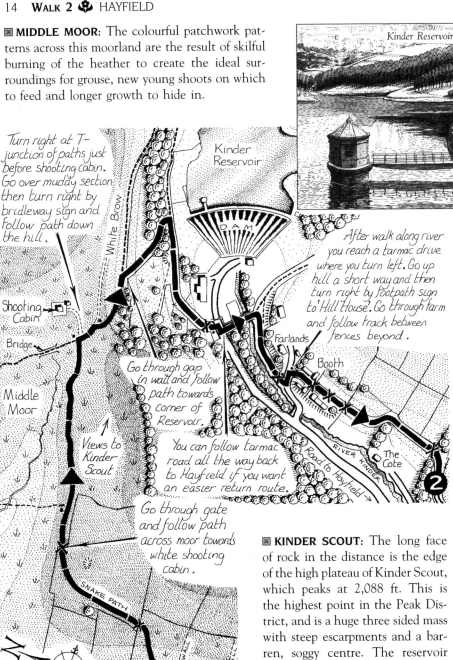

Kinder Reservoir

Kinder Reservoir

Turn right at T-junction of paths just before shooting cabin. Go over muddy section then turn right by bridleway sign and follow path down the hill.

White Brow

DAM

Shooting Cabin

Bridge

Middle Moor

Views to Kinder Scout

Go through gap in wall and follow path towards corner of Reservoir.

You can follow tarmac road all the way back to Hayfield if you want an easier return route.

Go through gate and follow path across moor towards white shooting cabin.

SNAKE PATH

N

OLD WALL

OLD WALL

Farlands

Booth

After walk along river you reach a tarmac drive where you turn left. Go up hill a short way and then turn right by footpath sign to 'Hill House'. Go through farm and follow track between fences beyond.

RIVER KINDER

Road to Hayfield →

The Cote

2

⊠ **KINDER SCOUT:** The long face of rock in the distance is the edge of the high plateau of Kinder Scout, which peaks at 2,088 ft. This is the highest point in the Peak District, and is a huge three sided mass with steep escarpments and a barren, soggy centre. The reservoir below was completed in 1911 and supplies water to Stockport.

1

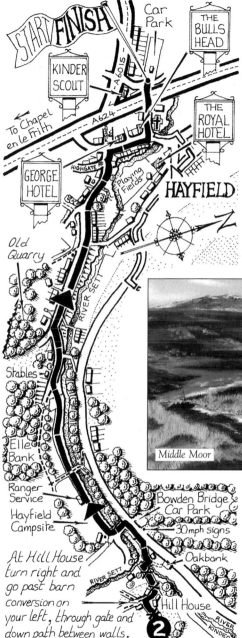

Scout on 24th April 1932 started here. The story goes that up to a thousand people, campaigning for greater access for ramblers, walked up past the reservoir, then burst through a line of gamekeepers and scrambled up to the summit. The truth is that the event was organised by a political group affiliated to the Communist Party, who were snubbed by rambling organisations at the time. About 200 people turned up, with just 40 or so attempting to climb up Kinder, and they only made a few hundred yards before turning back – they never reached the top. It was the harsh jail sentences handed out to the leaders that galvanised support for the campaign for public access.

Middle Moor

☒ **THE MASS TRESPASS:** Bowden Bridge car park has a memorial plaque to commemorate that the Mass Trespass of Kinder

REFRESHMENTS:
THE GEORGE HOTEL, Church Street, Hayfield. Open 12 noon to 3 pm and 5.30 pm to 11 pm on weekdays; 11 am to 11 pm on Saturday; 12 noon to 10.30 pm on Sunday. Telephone: 01663 743691.
THE ROYAL HOTEL, Market Street, Hayfield. Originally a vicarage dating from 1755. Open 12 noon to 3 pm and 6 pm to 11 pm on weekdays; 11 am to 11 pm on Saturday; 12 noon to 10.30 pm on Sunday. Telephone: 01663 742721.
THE SPORTSMAN, Kinder Road, Hayfield (opposite the stables on the map). Open 12 noon to 3 pm and 7 pm to 11 pm (closed Monday). Telephone: 01663 741565.

Walk 3
TAXAL
Length 3½ miles

Goyt Valley

The Peak District is still full of surprises. Away from the dramatic and popular attractions there are hidden valleys and secret villages free from the crowds and yet blessed with outstanding beauty. Here, only a few miles from the industrial fingers of Manchester, is a walk along the steep sided and heavily wooded Goyt valley, with the tiny hamlet of Taxal, just a few stone houses and an old church on a dead end lane, as your destination. Despite its remoteness, man's touch is never far away as the walk passes the old Cromford and High Peak Railway, and traverses the top of the dramatic Fernilee Reservoir. The return journey takes a higher route, past old farmhouses, down narrow gorges and over hills giving commanding views towards the distant Peaks.

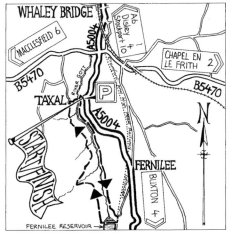

NB: There are no refreshments along this walk, so there will be a short drive at the end to Whaley Bridge.

it bends towards the river, go left through the small gate and along the footpath that runs through the wood. You follow this footpath above the left (east side) of the river all the way to Fernilee Reservoir.

▦ FERNILEE RESERVOIR: This flooded section of the Goyt valley was completed in 1938. At the same time the mixed deciduous and coniferous woodland that covers the west hillside was planted over previously open coun-

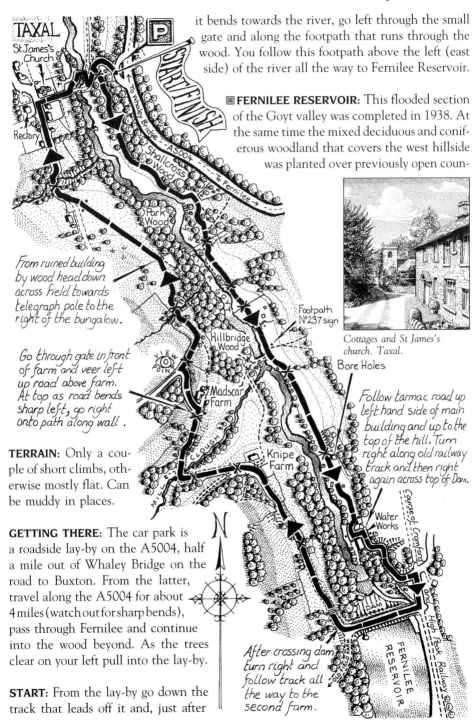

Cottages and St James's church. Taxal.

TERRAIN: Only a couple of short climbs, otherwise mostly flat. Can be muddy in places.

GETTING THERE: The car park is a roadside lay-by on the A5004, half a mile out of Whaley Bridge on the road to Buxton. From the latter, travel along the A5004 for about 4 miles (watch out for sharp bends), pass through Fernilee and continue into the wood beyond. As the trees clear on your left pull into the lay-by.

START: From the lay-by go down the track that leads off it and, just after

Map labels:

TAXAL
St James's Church
Rectory
P
To Whaley Bridge — A5004
STARTFINISH
Shallcross Wood
To Fernilee
Park Wood
RIVER GOYT
From ruined building by wood head down across field towards telegraph pole to the right of the bungalow.
Footpath Nº237 sign
Bore Holes
Hillbridge Wood
VIEW POINT
Go through gate in front of farm and veer left up road above farm. At top as road bends sharp left, go right onto path along wall.
Madscar Farm
Follow tarmac road up left hand side of main building and up to the top of the hill. Turn right along old railway track and then right again across top of Dam.
MILLER'S CLOUGH
Knipe Farm
Water Works
Course of Cromford
N
DAM
FERNILEE RESERVOIR
Course of Cromford and High Peak Railway
After crossing dam turn right and follow track all the way to the second farm.

Fernilee Reservoir

much of its length is now the High Peak Trail. The section here runs along the east bank of Fernilee Reservoir and at its southern end the road which crosses Errwood Dam runs up one of the old incline planes.

TAXAL: A picturesque hamlet of gritstone houses up to 300 years old around the church of St James. This edifice was originally known as St Leonard's and its tower dates from the 16th century, although the body of the church was rebuilt in 1825, and restored again in 1889. Inside is a tablet to Michael Heathcote, with an inscription that reads 'Gentleman of the Pantry and Yeoman of the Mouth to his late Majesty King George III'. It comes as a surprise when you walk down behind the church to find a huge graveyard with probably more headstones than there were people who ever lived in Taxal. The reason for this is that Whaley Bridge was originally a small settlement within the parish of Taxal and although with the coming of the canal it grew into a sizable little industrial town, St James's is still its parish church!

try. It is probably best not to worry anyone using the water that there is a flooded gunpowder mill beneath the reservoir!

⌗ **CROMFORD AND HIGH PEAK RAILWAY:** The problem when building canals is water supply, and the porous limestone hills in the Peak District made a route across them virtually impossible. Therefore, in order to link the Peak Forest Canal at Whaley Bridge with the Cromford Canal on the opposite side, and connect into the various quarries and mines en route, a tramway was built. It had horses to pull the wagons along the level sections and stationary steam engines to hoist them up the incline planes, which along with some alarming sharp bends allowed it to cross this hilly landscape. It was opened in 1830, though by 1841 the horses had been replaced by steam locomotives. It was used mainly for goods (which is not surprising as any passengers had to get out and walk up the incline planes) and its connection with the canals was demonstrated as the stations along its route were still known as wharves. The railway finally closed in the 1960s and

REFRESHMENTS:
As the Royal Oak in Taxal is no more, here are a few suggestions of places down the road in Whaley Bridge:
THE GOYT INN, Bridge Street (side street opposite station). Popular little pub with real fires in winter and wooden beams. Open 12 noon to 3 pm and 5 pm to 11 pm. Meals served at lunchtimes only. Telephone: 01663 732840.
THE SHEPHERD'S ARMS, Old Road (just above the A5004 in the town centre). Open 11 am to 11 pm; 12 noon to 10.30 pm on Sunday. Sandwiches served 12 noon to 4 pm (approx). Plenty of outside seating on terraces. Telephone: 01663 732384.
THE NAVIGATION INN, Johnson Street (near canal wharf). Open 11 am to 11 pm; 12 noon to 10.30 pm on Sunday. Food served 12 noon to 4 pm daily. Telephone: 01663 732308.

Walk 4
CASTLETON AND MAM TOR
Length 5 miles

Peveril Castle, Castleton

*F*ew places in England can match Castleton for such an entertaining mix of drama, mystery, history and shopping! There are its numerous caves and mines, the mighty Peveril Castle, the imposing Mam Tor with its views over Edale and the charming old stone town with its pubs, cafés and unique jewellery shops. Not only does this walk encompass many of these features, but it also passes the huge landslide that closed the old A625, the windswept Iron Age hillfort on the summit of Mam Tor and the dramatic limestone cliffs of Winnats Pass.

NB: Castleton can get very busy at weekends and in the school holidays. The earlier you start the better!

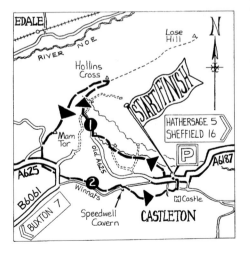

TERRAIN: There is a steady climb of over 2 miles up to Mam Tor (1,000 ft). The path up to Hollins Cross can be very muddy in places.

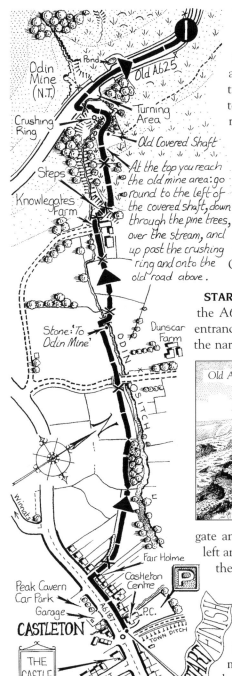

GETTING THERE: Castleton sits almost at the centre of the Peak District. From Buxton take the A6, signposted to Stockport, and after passing through Dove Holes turn right at the roundabout onto the A623, and then after a mile turn left down the side of the Wanted Inn towards Castleton. A couple of miles on turn right towards Peveril Castle and go down through Winnats Pass until at the T-junction you turn right into Castleton. At the mini roundabout turn left into the main car park (fee payable). From Sheffield and the east take the A625 up onto the moors and then keep on the same road as it becomes the A6187 all the way to Castleton, where you turn right at the mini roundabout just past the Castle Hotel into the car park.

START: From the car park entrance turn right up the A6187 towards Winnats and then just past the entrance to the Peak Cavern car park turn right up the narrow path between the houses. Go through the

Old A625 landslip

gate and keep to the path along the hedge on your left and follow the signs to Mam Tor until you reach the old A625 just past Odin Mine.

▨ **ODIN MINE**: References to poaching around the entrance of Odin from 1280 make this the oldest named mine in Derbyshire. It was in the 18th century though that large-scale mining took place and the network of shafts and levels were expanded in the search for lead until it was wound down in the early 19th century.

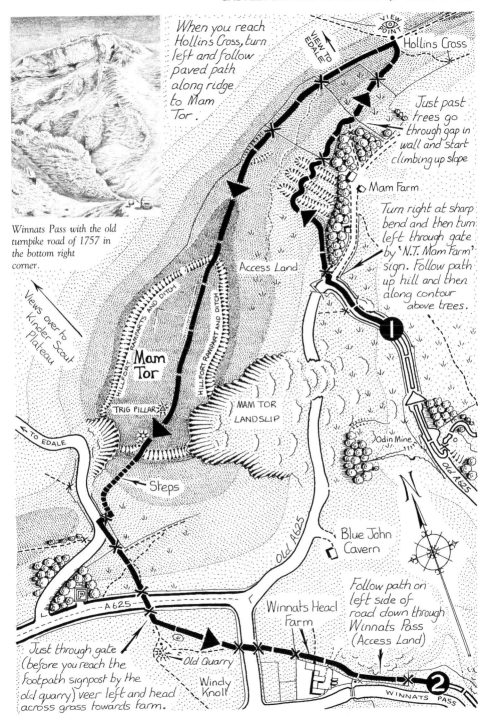

When you reach Hollins Cross, turn left and follow paved path along ridge to Mam Tor.

Hollins Cross

VIEW POINT

VIEW TO EDALE

Just past trees go through gap in wall and start climbing up slope

Mam Farm

Turn right at sharp bend and then turn left through gate by 'N.T. Mam Farm' sign. Follow path up hill and then along contour above trees.

1

Winnats Pass with the old turnpike road of 1757 in the bottom right corner.

Access Land

Views over to Kinder Scout Plateau

HILLFORT RAMPARTS AND DITCH

HILLFORT RAMPART AND DITCH

Mam Tor

TRIG PILLAR

TO EDALE

MAM TOR LANDSLIP

Odin Mine

Old A625

N

Steps

Old A625

Blue John Cavern

Follow path on left side of road down through Winnats Pass (Access Land)

P

A625

Old Quarry

Windy Knoll

Winnats Head Farm

2

WINNATS PASS

Just through gate (before you reach the footpath signpost by the old quarry) veer left and head across grass towards farm.

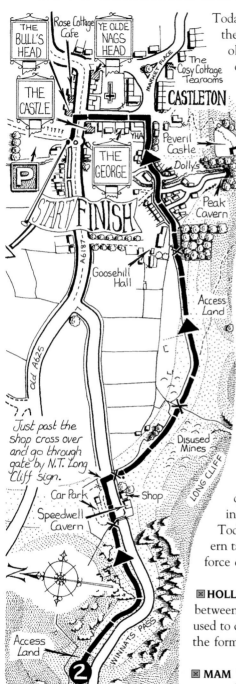

Today the narrow gorge above the A625 marks the entrance to the mine, while below it the old crushing circle marks the area where the ore (or 'booze') was ground down and separated by sieving and washing in the stream.

⊠ **MAM TOR LANDSLIP**: The eastern face of this hill has been slipping away due to its fragile sandwich of shales for at least 3,000 years, so it is a surprise that the Manchester–Sheffield Turnpike Trust decided to run their new road over it in 1802. Despite fre-

Castleton with Peak Cavern in the rear

quent repairs the road was finally abandoned in 1979 after a major slip two years earlier. Today you can see the alarming sight of a modern tarmac road buckled and ripped apart by the force of nature.

⊠ **HOLLINS CROSS**: This low point along the ridge between Lose Hill and Mam Tor was on the route used to carry coffins from Edale to Castleton before the former had its own chapel.

⊠ **MAM TOR HILLFORT**: The bank and ditch that surrounded this 16 acre defensive settlement on the top of Mam Tor are crossed by the footpath as you

A view from the ridge top walk between Hollins Cross and Mam Tor looking down on Edale with the plateau of Kinder Scout in the distance. This ridge marks the boundary between the limestone to the south and the millstone grit to the north. The remote valley below has long been farmed by man, the word 'booth' in the place names implies that they were once used as shelters in summer.

⊠ **BLUE JOHN MINE AND TREAK CLIFF CAVERN:** The semi-precious stone known as Blue John is fluorspar with amethyst or topaz colouring and the only workable quantities are found at these two sites (the later being discovered as recently as 1926). As the land is now owned by the National Trust only limited working is permitted.

⊠ **WINNATS PASS:** Although it looks as if it had been carved out by a river, this dramatic gorge is probably a gap between ancient coral reefs when the limestone was formed in tropical seas some 300 million years ago. The name is believed to come from 'Windy Gates' and the road that runs down here was the original turnpike route dating from 1757 before the new road over the Mam Tor Landslip bypassed it in 1802.

⊠ **SPEEDWELL CAVERN:** Principally a lead mine, which was expanded in 1774 when an underground canal was dug to bring the ore out from deep inside. Although it was abandoned soon after, tourists can now take boat trips along the underground waterway.

⊠ **PEAK CAVERN:** Unlike the other underground attractions in the area this cave is natural, with its huge, gaping entrance listed as one of the Seven Wonders of the Peaks back in the 16th century. Known by locals as the 'Devil's Hole or Arse', it was the home to rope-makers as the damp conditions where the Peakshole Water emerges created the constant humidity they required.

approach and descend the summit. There is some doubt as to the age of the site, which radiocarbon dating has put at around 1180 BC, much earlier than most hillforts, which tend to be from 600 BC to AD 43. It was in this period that the defences were strengthened with stone reinforcement of the rampart and extra ditches and banks around the vulnerable south-west entrance. The platforms on which their circular houses stood can still be found around the outer edges of the site. Some hillforts were permanently occupied and acted as market centres for Iron Age tribes while others were probably used principally as a refuge and it is fair to assume that this site falls into the latter category as you can imagine what the weather is like up here in winter!

⊠ **WINDY KNOLL:** A disused limestone quarry stands here, just behind an old cave entrance in which have been found the bones of rhinos, bears and wolves dating from before the last Ice Age.

The view below is of Mam Tor from Peveril Castle. The zig-zag pattern in the wall on the left is one of the earliest surviving parts.

❊ **PEVERIL CASTLE:** Iron Age hillforts were last ditch defences for a community, whereas the medieval castles were jointly a home for their owner and a stronghold from which he could control the local people and trade. This is why William Peveril built his castle here in 1068 on a prominent rock down in the valley rather than re-using the old hillfort on Mam Tor – not only could he keep a close eye on the unruly Saxons and protect the lead mines, but also he wasn't too far from water and food in case of a siege. The herringbone pattern (zig-zag) of stone in the west wall dates from this early phase of its history. Unfortunately in the civil unrest of King Stephen's reign the fourth William Peveril was accused of attempting to poison the Earl of Chester and in 1153 had his castle and lands forfeited to the Crown. The new monarch, Henry II, received the submission of Malcolm, King of the Scots here in 1157 and spent money strengthening the castle including building the keep. It had started to lose its importance by the 14th century, in common with most castles – there was little military threat away from the Borders and the coastline and the gentry required more luxurious residences than could be provided by these cold lofty towers.

❊ **CASTLETON:** For all its quaint rustic appearance, Castleton is a planned town, a medieval mini Milton Keynes! It was laid out to a grid plan probably in the 1170s at the same time that Peveril Castle was being rebuilt, and, with the addition of a market that was granted in 1222, was intended as a financial investment from rents and tolls as much as a home for the local workforce. At its centre is St Edmund's church, which still retains the original 12th century chancel arch with its distinctive zig-zag decoration, while around the outside, sections of the town's defensive ditch can still be traced (one length is between the Bull's Head and the main car park). Thankfully, Castleton never developed into a large settlement, although it still has a few buildings with grand ambitions, most notably the Youth Hostel, which is a 17th century hall with a rather clumsy attempt at Classical decoration.

REFRESHMENTS:

There are numerous hotels, pubs, restaurants and tea rooms in Castleton, including:

THE GEORGE HOTEL, Castle Street. Open 11 am to 11 pm in summer (12 noon to 10.30 pm on Sunday) and 12 noon to 3 pm and 6 pm to 11 pm in winter. Telephone: 01433 620238.

THE CASTLE HOTEL, Castle Street. Open 11 am to 11 pm (12 noon to 10.30 pm on Sunday). Telephone: 01433 620578.

THE BULL'S HEAD, Cross Street. Open 11 am to 11 pm (12 noon to 10.30 pm on Sunday). Telephone: 01433 620256.

YE OLDE NAGS HEAD, Cross Street. Open 9 am to 9 pm. Telephone: 01433 620248.

ROSE COTTAGE CAFE, Cross Street. Open 10am to 5 pm (closed Fridays and through January and February). Telephone: 01433 620472.

THREE ROOFS CAFE (opposite entrance to main car park). Open 10am to 5 pm on Monday to Friday; 9.30 am to 5.30 pm at weekends. Telephone: 01433 620533.

HATHERSAGE AND STANAGE EDGE
Length 5½ miles

North Lees

This area around the ancient village of Hathersage is steeped in history, from the mysterious earthworks at Camp Green and the old Roman road high on Stanage Edge to the Tudor Tower House of North Lees on the edge of the moors. Two famous stories have their links here, the grave of Robin Hood's famous stick-wielding companion Little John lies in the churchyard, while the village under the guise of 'Morton' was the setting for Charlotte Brontë's 'Jane Eyre'. This circular walk not only uncovers these notable places but also takes you through an ever changing landscape to the jagged crest of Stanage Edge.

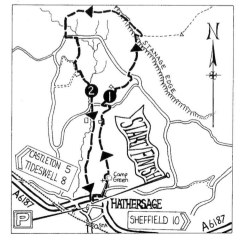

NB: You can shorten the route by cutting across Birley Lane just before point 1.

TERRAIN: A long steady climb of about 800 ft over 2 miles up to Stanage Edge. Paths are generally good, although a bit vague and muddy in places.

GETTING THERE: Hathersage is 10 miles west of Sheffield on the A6187. Head out of the city on the A625 and then just

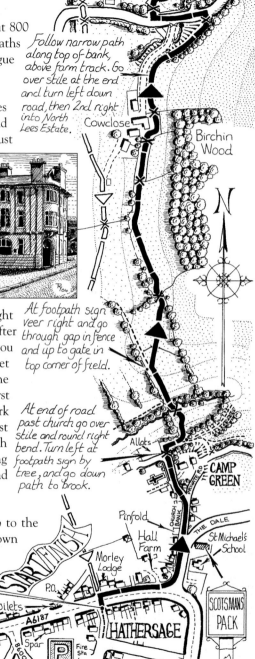

Follow narrow path along top of bank, above farm track. Go over stile at the end and turn left down road, then 2nd right into North Lees Estate.

after entering the Peak District veer right onto the A6187 towards Castleton. After 3 miles you reach Hathersage, where you turn left at the bottom of Main Street opposite the George Inn (following the parking signs) and then take your first left up to the pay and display car park just before the right bend. From the west the best approach is via the B6049 north from Tideswell, and then turn right along the A6187 at the T-junction beyond Brough and continue to Hathersage.

At footpath sign veer right and go through gap in fence and up to gate in top corner of field.

At end of road past church go over stile and round right bend. Turn left at footpath sign by tree, and go down path to brook.

START: From the car park turn left up to the right hand bend but carry straight on down the path that leads to the main street. Turn right up the hill and then left at the top just before the main road bends to the right. Go down past the school and then veer left opposite the Scotsman's Pack up Church Bank. At the top turn left and follow the road round past the church.

⊠ **CAMP GREEN:** These earthworks, which comprise the remains of a circular ditch and bank, are of unknown origin; some believe they date from the Iron Age, others associate them with the Danes. With its position on a low promontory next to the church the site is more likely to be that of an early ringwork castle (one surrounded by ditches and banks but with no motte) dating from the 11th or 12th century.

⊠ **ST MICHAEL'S CHURCH:** This attractively set church, which dates from the late 14th century, owes much to its restoration in 1849–52 and to the addition in 1949 of stained glass by Kempe in its east window. This came from the church at Derwent shortly before it vanished under the new reservoir. In the churchyard is the grave of Little John, one of Robin Hood's companions. When this was opened in 1784 a

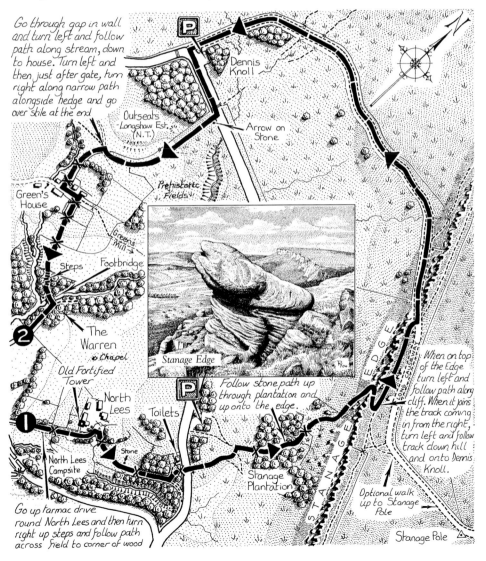

Go through gap in wall and turn left and follow path along stream, down to house. Turn left and then, just after gate, turn right along narrow path alongside hedge and go over stile at the end

Dennis Knoll

Outseats Longshaw Est. (N.T.)

Arrow on Stone

Green's House

Prehistoric Fields

Green's Mill

Steps

Footbridge

The Warren

⚓ Chapel

Old Fortified Tower

North Lees

Toilets

Stanage Edge

Follow stone path up through plantation and up onto the edge.

When on top of the Edge turn left and follow path along cliff. When it joins the track coming in from the right, turn left and follow track down hill and onto Dennis Knoll.

North Lees Campsite

Stone

Stanage Plantation

Optional walk up to Stanage Pole

Go up tarmac drive round North Lees and then turn right up steps and follow path across field to corner of wood

Stanage Pole

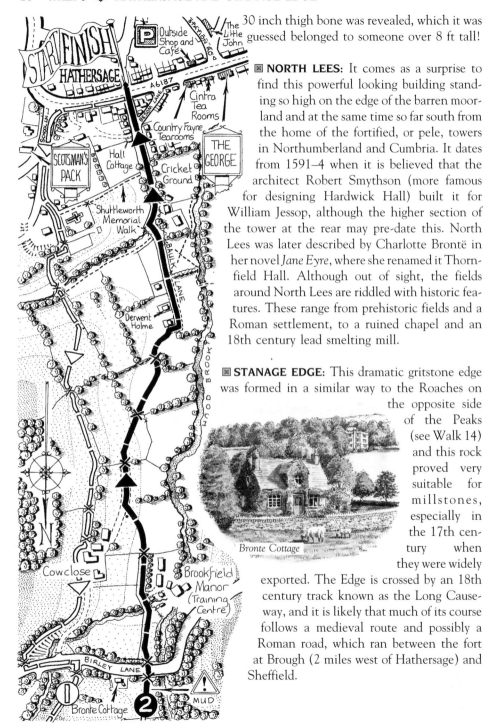

30 inch thigh bone was revealed, which it was guessed belonged to someone over 8 ft tall!

▣ **NORTH LEES:** It comes as a surprise to find this powerful looking building standing so high on the edge of the barren moorland and at the same time so far south from the home of the fortified, or pele, towers in Northumberland and Cumbria. It dates from 1591–4 when it is believed that the architect Robert Smythson (more famous for designing Hardwick Hall) built it for William Jessop, although the higher section of the tower at the rear may pre-date this. North Lees was later described by Charlotte Brontë in her novel *Jane Eyre*, where she renamed it Thornfield Hall. Although out of sight, the fields around North Lees are riddled with historic features. These range from prehistoric fields and a Roman settlement, to a ruined chapel and an 18th century lead smelting mill.

▣ **STANAGE EDGE:** This dramatic gritstone edge was formed in a similar way to the Roaches on the opposite side of the Peaks (see Walk 14) and this rock proved very suitable for millstones, especially in the 17th century when they were widely exported. The Edge is crossed by an 18th century track known as the Long Causeway, and it is likely that much of its course follows a medieval route and possibly a Roman road, which ran between the fort at Brough (2 miles west of Hathersage) and Sheffield.

Bronte Cottage

⊠ **BROOKFIELD MANOR:** Behind its Victorian façade of 1870 is a building dating from the 16th century; unfortunately today it is a private training centre so only a glimpse is possible.

⊠**HATHERSAGE:** An important centre from Saxon times, possibly around the Camp Green area, which was said to be occupied by the first Norman holders of the manor. The village grew as a result of its industry, especially the drawing of wire to make needles and nails, a trade that was brought here by Christopher Schutz from Germany in 1566. In addition to this there was papermaking (the water off the moors being pure enough for the process to take place at Green's Mill near North Lees), lead smelting (which took place at Green's Mill before it was converted to paper-making in the 19th century) and the production of saws. Charlotte Brontë stayed at the vicarage in 1845 and in *Jane Eyre* the character St John Rivers is said to be based on the then vicar Henry Hussey, and Morton

is Hathersage (Morton was apparently the name of the landlord of the George at the time). Today it is an excellent centre for exploring the surrounding hills and moors and is well equipped with shops, cafés and tearooms.

REFRESHMENTS:

THE SCOTSMAN'S PACK, School Lane, Hathersage. Open 11 am to 11 pm on Saturday; 12 noon to 10.30 pm on Sunday; 11.30 am to 3 pm and 6 pm to 11 pm in the week. It may be worth booking if you want to eat here at weekends. Telephone: 01433 630253.

THE LITTLE JOHN HOTEL, Station Road, Hathersage. Open 11 am to 11 pm (12 noon to 10.30 pm on Sunday). Telephone: 01433 630225.

CINTRA'S RESTAURANT AND TEA ROOMS, Main Street, Hathersage. Open 8.30 am to 6 pm daily in summer and 9.30 am to 4.30 pm in winter. Full range of hot and cold food including breakfasts, and a tea garden at the rear. Telephone: 01433 651825.

COUNTRY FAYRE TEA ROOM, Main Street, Hathersage. Open approx 11 am to 5 pm through the summer and at weekends in winter. Telephone: 01433 650858.

Stanage Edge

Eyam

The tragic story of the devastating plague and the villagers' noble efforts to restrict it within the parish is the principal reason why tourists flock to this corner of the Peaks. The tale has an added dimension as many of the places and sites associated with the events of 1665 still stand today. Yet there is much more to Eyam and the surrounding countryside, some things of far greater antiquity like the beautifully carved cross in the churchyard, which is around 1100 years old, others like the old lead mines of a more recent industrial age. This walk takes in many aspects of this attractive stone built village and the high moor above, where amidst the stunning views there are reminders of the tragedy that befell this isolated community.

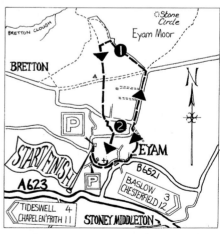

NB: Eyam can be very busy on summer weekends and bank holidays.

TERRAIN: One steep climb out of the village, 350 ft. It can be muddy on the moor.

GETTING THERE: Eyam is just off the A623 between Peak Forest and Baslow. From Buxton take the A6 north towards Chapel en le Frith and then turn right onto the A623 at the roundabout just after Dove Holes. Continue for about 10 miles, then turn left up the B6521 into Eyam. Take your first left, then go left again along Church Street (following the parking signs). Just past the hall turn right and the main car park is opposite the museum (pay and display). From the east use the A619 Bakewell to Chesterfield road and turn onto the A623 at Baslow. Continue north for about 3 miles and then turn right onto the B6521 and follow the above instructions to reach the car park.

START: From the car park turn left back down Hawkhill Road, turn left at the bottom and follow this road past the hall and church, through the centre of the village and out as far as the old Wesleyan chapel,

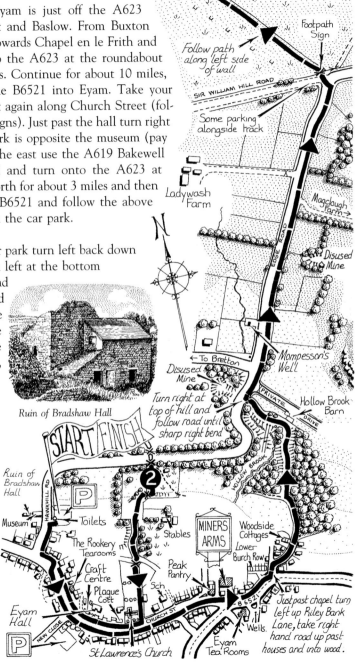

Eyam's Saxon cross

Ruin of Bradshaw Hall

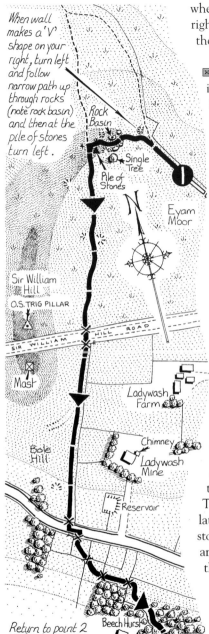

When wall makes a 'V' shape on your right, turn left and follow narrow path up through rocks (note rock basin) and then at the pile of stones turn left.

Sir William Hill
O.S. TRIG PILLAR

Single Tree
Pile of Stones
Rock Basin
Eyam Moor

Mast
Bole Hill
Ladywash Farm
Chimney
Ladywash Mine
Reservoir

Return to point 2 on first map and follow route down hill towards church, and back onto main road via the churchyard.

Beech Hurst
YHA

where you turn left up Riley Bank Lane. Take the right hand fork, up past the houses and then follow the path up into the woods beyond.

❉ EYAM: Pronounced E'em, this old mining village is believed to date as far back as the 9th century, its name probably coming from 'ey' for water and 'ham' meaning settlement, as this is the point where water emerges from beneath the sandstone edge. In 1588 a series of troughs connected by pipes were fed by this spring water to become one of the earliest known public water supplies and parts of this network still survive in the village today. More attractive are the well dressings, a tradition that is believed to date back to the 17th century at least and was revived here in 1951.

❉ THE PLAGUE: The Bubonic Plague and the more virulent Pneumonic Plague had been endemic in Britain since the Black Death of 1348/49 especially in densely populated urban areas. The final epidemic in this country, the Great Plague, occurred in 1665/66, principally in London but also in Norwich, Southampton and Newcastle. The story about Eyam tells how a tailor, George Viccars, ordered cloth from London which unknown to him contained fleas carrying the bacterium and from his lodgings at Plague Cottage next to the church the disease spread through the village, but not before the rector William Mompesson and his predecessor Thomas Stanley had convinced the locals to isolate themselves from the outside world. This famous story of sacrifice is retold in detail within the church and museum, while plaques on various houses throughout the village record the distressing loss of

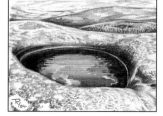

The rock basin on Eyam Moor. Some were natural, others drilled into boulders and then filled with vinegar so that money left for supplies would be disinfected (or so it was believed at the time).

Eyam Moor

life at these properties. It is still unknown today why the plague never returned after this outbreak, but it is now believed that the sort of quarantine action taken by Eyam was also being repeated across Europe and played its part in the sudden demise of the epidemic.

▨ **BRADSHAW HALL:** A house begun by George Bradshaw in 1635 but never completed due to the Civil War and his death. One fragment of the ruins stands behind the museum.

▨ **EYAM HALL:** This solid looking manor house dates from 1676 and has been in the hands of the Wright family ever since.

▨ **EYAM CROSS AND ST LAWRENCE'S CHURCH:** The Saxon cross with its carvings of trumpet-playing angels and spiralling foliage dates from the early 9th century but was originally elsewhere, possibly opposite the hall where the stocks stand. It had been removed, probably in the 17th century, and was rediscovered lying in the churchyard in 1778 and reset in its current position minus the top 2 ft of the shaft. The church is also worth investigating, especially for the wall paintings inside and the huge sundial on the south of the chancel wall.

▨ **MOMPESSON'S WELL:** One of the appointed places where supplies could be left, since named after the rector.

▨ **LEAD MINES:** The remains of lead mines largely abandoned by the late 19th century can be seen along the route, most notably New Engine Mine which had a shaft of 1092 ft, the deepest of any lead mine in Derbyshire. A few, including Ladywash, have still been working recently extracting fluorspar for use in the steel, ceramic and chemical industries.

REFRESHMENTS:
THE MINERS ARMS, Water Lane, Eyam. Claims to be one of the most haunted pubs in the Peaks! Open 11 am to 11 pm (12 noon to 10.30 pm on Sunday). Telephone: 01433 630853.
EYAM TEA ROOMS, The Square, Eyam. Open 10 am to 5 pm daily (4 pm in winter). Hot and cold meals. Telephone: 01433 631274.
THE ROOKERY, Main Road, Eyam. Open 10 am to 5 pm daily (4.30 pm in winter). Hot and cold meals. Telephone: 01433 639666.

TIDESWELL
Length 5 miles

St John the Baptist Church, Tideswell

It comes as a surprise to find tucked away in a quiet dale only a few miles from busy Buxton another ancient town but one barely touched by the Industrial Revolution. Tideswell's loss in the 19th century is its gain today, as its medieval layout has survived with an elongated market place flanked by rustic stone cottages, a number of grand 18th century buildings and at its head a most impressive parish church, rightly known as the 'Cathedral of the Peaks'. In contrast this walk passes over ancient fields to Miller's Dale, an area that was shaped by the very industrialists who passed Tideswell by. Although it is a beautiful wooded valley today, the scars of the past are still visible under this attractive veneer and the stories of its harsh life are still fresh in the mind.

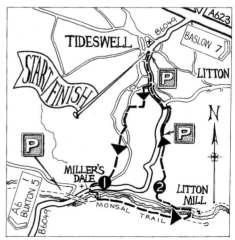

TERRAIN: Only two short climbs as most of the ascent is spread out over the return along Tideswell Dale and is hardly noticeable. NB: The first part of the walk is not clear on the ground – see notes alongside map.

GETTING THERE: From Buxton head out towards Matlock on the A6 for about 4 miles until, after climbing out of the Wye valley, you turn left down the B6049 to Tideswell. Pass through Miller's Dale and on into the town, where parking is either in a small area in the centre near the toilets or along the main road.

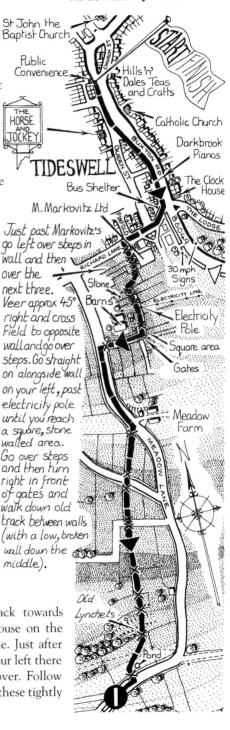

St John the
Baptist Church

Public
Convenience

Hills 'n'
Dales Teas
and Crafts

THE
HORSE
AND
JOCKEY

Catholic Church

Darkbrook
Pianos

TIDESWELL

The Clock
House

Bus Shelter

M. Markovitz Ltd

Just past Markovitz's
go left over steps in
wall and then
over the
next three.
Veer approx 45°
right and cross
field to opposite
wall and go over
steps. Go straight
on alongside wall
on your left, past
electricity pole
until you reach
a square, stone
walled area.
Go over steps
and then turn
right in front
of gates and
walk down old
track between walls
(with a low, broken
wall down the
middle).

Stone
Barns

30 mph
Signs

ELECTRICITY LINE

Electricity
Pole

Square area

Gates

Meadow
Farm

N

Old
Lynchets

Pond

Miller's Dale

START: From your parking place head back towards Miller's Dale and then opposite the last house on the left (Clock House) go right up Richard Lane. Just after the concrete drive to M. Markovitz Ltd on your left there is a step in the stone wall, which you go over. Follow the notes and map to track the footpath over these tightly packed fields.

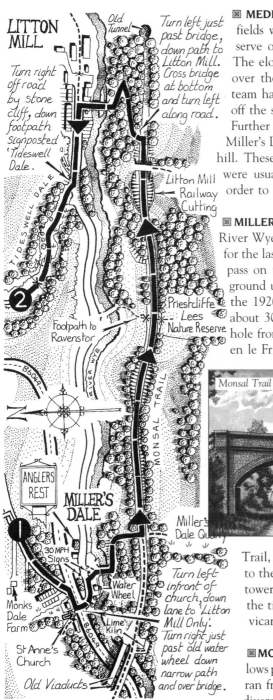

LITTON MILL

Old Tunnel

Turn right off road by stone cliff, down footpath signposted 'Tideswell Dale'.

Turn left just past bridge, down path to Litton Mill. Cross bridge at bottom and turn left along road.

Litton Mill
← Railway
Cutting

2

Footpath to Ravenstor

Priestcliffe ⚘
⚘ Lees ⚘
Nature Reserve

ANGLERS REST

MILLER'S DALE

Miller's Dale Quarry

30 MPH Signs

Water Wheel

Monks Dale Farm

Lime Kiln

St Anne's Church

Old Viaducts

Turn left in front of church, down lane to 'Litton Mill Only'.
Turn right just past old water wheel down narrow path and over bridge.

☒ **MEDIEVAL FIELDS:** These long, narrow fields with slightly curved stone walls preserve old strips from medieval open fields. The elongated S shape formed by the walls over their length was the path the plough team had to take in order to turn onto and off the strip all those hundreds of years ago. Further along as you begin to drop down in Miller's Dale there are steps in the side of the hill. These are probably strip lynchets, which were usually formed in medieval farming in order to plough sloping land.

☒ **MILLER'S DALE:** This hamlet alongside the River Wye has been home to at least one mill for the last 900 years. The old water wheel you pass on this walk powered millstones which ground up meal for animal feed. It closed in the 1920s and the building was demolished about 30 years ago to make way for a borehole from which water is pumped to Chapel en le Frith (from the small building next to it). The wooded valley hides the old limestone quarry, which was opened up on a large scale with the arrival of the railway in 1863. Today it is a nature reserve on the other side of the Monsal Trail, but the old limekilns still stand next to the viaducts. St Anne's church with its tower set to one side, seemingly to fit into the tight site, was designed by Tideswell's vicar in 1880.

Monsal Trail

☒ **MONSAL TRAIL:** This popular track follows part of the old Midland railway, which ran from London to Manchester. A short diversion from the walk takes you back to the two viaducts with dramatic views down Miller's Dale. The one you walk across was the original, built in 1863, the other was opened in 1905 to cope with an increase in traffic. Nearby are steps leading up to the well-preserved limekilns, which were built in 1878. There are information boards at points along the trail. Look out for the one explaining the 330 million year old lava flow in Litton Mill railway cutting.

⊞ LITTON MILL: Another settlement based around mills and quarrying, which has evolved with weathering and the encroachment of nature into an attractive riverside hamlet. The mill, which has recently been converted into flats, has a less appealing past. In the 1830s when the exploitation of child labour was coming to national attention, Litton Mill was exposed for the cruelty of its owners Ellis Needham and Sons. Even at nearby Cressbrook Mill, which was praised by some for its more humane approach, orphans as young as 10 were put to work from 6 am to 8 pm with only an hour's break for lunch, most of which was spent oiling machinery! Many were beaten and abused, sadly some dying as a result, their bodies being quietly buried in unmarked graves at Tideswell. The original mill of 1782 in which these cruel acts took place burnt down and was replaced by the present structure in 1874.

⊞ TIDESWELL DALE: A limestone valley, which like Miller's Dale contains layers of volcanic rock from eruptions in the tropical seas that 330 million years ago covered the area of the Peak District. This basalt is used for road surfacing and an outcrop was quarried in the dale, leaving behind a flat sill that is now a lofty picnic site.

⬛ **TIDESWELL:** Although it is not certain if it was named after a Saxon called Tidi, or because of the habit of wells in the area to ebb and flow like the tide, it is known that by the 14th century Tideswell was an important and prosperous town and a centre for the Royal Peak Forest, with Edward I visiting here in 1275. A clear reflection of its status is the church of St John the Baptist, not only impressive in size and rich in ornament but unlike most parish churches, which are a collection of parts from different periods, it was built over some seventy years during the 14th century and retains its original unity. Even in this short time, though, there were changing fashions, which you can see in the difference between the elaborate flowing tracery (stone bars) of the Decorated style (1320–50) in the windows of the nave and transept, compared with the tall, square headed ones in the chancel (1360–80), heralding a change to the Perpendicular. Inside are notable memorials, including the tomb of Sir Sampson Meverill in the cen-

tre of the chancel, which – like many 15th century memorials – has a decomposed statue of the deceased (a cadaver) underneath the top. It's worth exploring the back lanes of Tideswell with its many fine 18th century buildings including the George Hotel, notable for its Venetian windows. The town is also rare in having a Cow Club, which was set up to fund insurance for vet bills, and remarkably has survived to be the only one of its kind in the country.

REFRESHMENTS:
THE GEORGE HOTEL, Commercial Road, Tideswell. Popular old coaching inn dating from 1730. Open 10.30 am to 3 pm and 7 pm to 11 pm (12 noon to 3 pm on Sunday). Telephone: 01298 871382.
THE HORSE AND JOCKEY, Queen Street, Tideswell. Open 10.30 am to 3 pm and 7 pm to 11 pm (12 noon to 3 pm on Sunday). Telephone: 01298 871597.
THE ANGLER'S REST, Miller's Dale. Open 12 noon to 3 pm and 6.30 pm to 11 pm. Telephone: 01298 871323.
HILLS 'N' DALES, Teas and Crafts, Tideswell. Open 10 am to 5 pm on Friday to Sunday, all year round.

Litton Mill

FOREST CHAPEL
Length 5 miles

Shutlingsloe from Macclesfield Forest

Only a mile or two away from the weekend hoards milling around the Goyt valley is a far more tranquil proposition. The tiny hamlet of Forest Chapel and the valley of Clough Brook below are a patchwork of lush pasture and woodland with the barren moorland and dramatic peaks of Shining Tor and Shutlingsloe looming above. This walk has many contrasting aspects, from the small, isolated farms and rustic chapel to the surprisingly massive old mill office in Wildboarclough, and from the peaceful pine strewn tracks through Macclesfield Forest to the hard stone paths and colourful grassland that covers the hills. There are some of the most spectacular views in the Peaks, some of the remotest buildings and two of the best pubs, standing at each end of this rewarding walk.

TERRAIN: One climb spread over a mile to Shutlingsloe, and two shorter ones. A mile or so of road walking. Some paths may be slippery or have a loose surface.

GETTING THERE: From Buxton take the A537 to Macclesfield and as you come down the hill after the Cat and Fiddle pub, take the first left turn just before the old quarry. At the bottom turn left opposite the Stanley Arms and then turn right up the narrow road to Forest Chapel. Ignore the right turn and carry on up to the top where the Standing Stone car park is on your right. From Macclesfield take the A537 towards Buxton and then a ⅓ of a mile after Walker Barn take the first right (in effect straight on) and follow it down to the Stanley Arms, where you turn right and then right again up the Forest Chapel road to the car park. NB: Standing Stone car park is small. If it is full, head down towards Wildboarclough and there are three other car parks alongside the road where you can pick up the walk.

START: From the car park, turn right onto the road up to the T-junction and then go through the gate on the opposite side and follow the path beyond along the edge of Macclesfield Forest and then down into it.

⊞**MACCLESFIELD FOREST:** This was once a Royal Hunting Ground, in effect a medieval game reserve for deer, which spread from the Dane and Goyt valleys in the east to Macclesfield in the west.

Arrow on stone
Shutlingsloe
Trig Pillar
VIEW POINT
ALTERNATIVE LOW ROUTE

Turn right and walk along fence up to the top of the hill. If you don't want to do the final part of the climb then follow the path around the base of Shutlingsloe.

Plank walkway
Stone Slab Path
HIGHMOOR BROOK
Seat
Macc Forest Sign

As you reach top corner of the forest and the path veers off to the right, go to your left up a faint path to the gate ahead.

VIEW POINT
Ferriser (ruins)
Pond
Macclesfield Forest
START/FINISH
WILDBOARCLOUGH
P
LANGLEY
Standing Stone

Shutlingsloe

Although the name would imply otherwise there was not necessarily any forest and it was probably an area of woodland, moorland and pasture that came under Forest Law, a set of rules to protect the animals and their surroundings from encroachments and poachers. In this period the

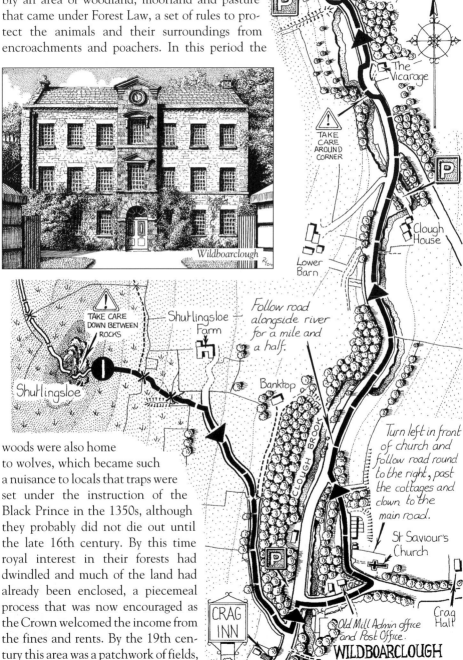

Wildboarclough

woods were also home to wolves, which became such a nuisance to locals that traps were set under the instruction of the Black Prince in the 1350s, although they probably did not die out until the late 16th century. By this time royal interest in their forests had dwindled and much of the land had already been enclosed, a piecemeal process that was now encouraged as the Crown welcomed the income from the fines and rents. By the 19th century this area was a patchwork of fields,

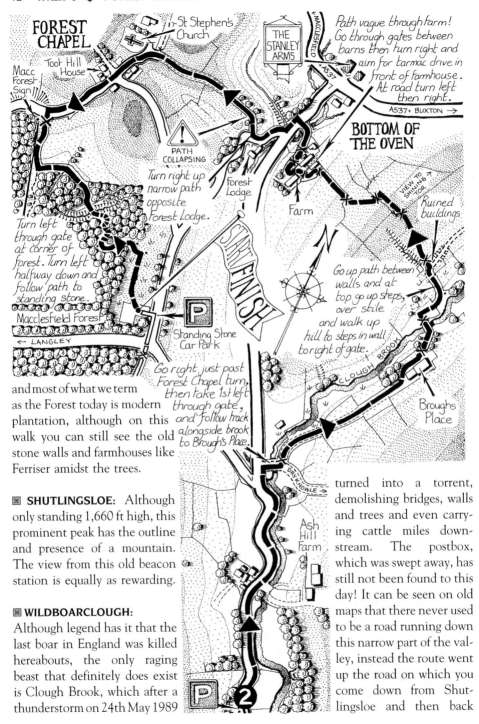

FOREST CHAPEL

Macc Forest Sign

Toot Hill House

St Stephen's Church

THE STANLEY ARMS

Path vague through farm! Go through gates between barns then turn right and aim for tarmac drive in front of farmhouse. At road turn left then right.

A537 → BUXTON →

BOTTOM OF THE OVEN

⚠ PATH COLLAPSING

Turn right up narrow path opposite Forest Lodge.

Forest Lodge

Farm

VIEW TO SHINING TOR →

Ruined buildings

Turn left through gate at corner of forest. Turn left halfway down and follow path to standing stone.

Macclesfield Forest

← LANGLEY

Go up path between walls and at top go up steps, over stile and walk up hill to steps in wall to right of gate.

SARVENISH

Ⓟ Standing Stone Car Park

Go right, just past Forest Chapel turn, then take 1st left through gate and follow track alongside brook to Brough's Place.

CLOUGH BROOK

Broughs Place

DRY KNOWLE →

Ash Hill Farm

Ⓟ ②

and most of what we term as the Forest today is modern plantation, although on this walk you can still see the old stone walls and farmhouses like Ferriser amidst the trees.

▣ **SHUTLINGSLOE:** Although only standing 1,660 ft high, this prominent peak has the outline and presence of a mountain. The view from this old beacon station is equally as rewarding.

▣ **WILDBOARCLOUGH:** Although legend has it that the last boar in England was killed hereabouts, the only raging beast that definitely does exist is Clough Brook, which after a thunderstorm on 24th May 1989 turned into a torrent, demolishing bridges, walls and trees and even carrying cattle miles downstream. The postbox, which was swept away, has still not been found to this day! It can be seen on old maps that there never used to be a road running down this narrow part of the valley, instead the route went up the road on which you come down from Shutlingsloe and then back down to join the brook at Clough House, possibly because of the turbulent nature of the brook. The wooded ravine in which this picturesque hamlet is hidden covers other scars, including the ruins of Crag Mill, which dominated this area in the late 18th and early 19th century. Parts of the foundations can still be seen under the trees on the opposite bank just before the bridge, while the impressive mill administration office (*circa* 1770), which later became the largest sub post office in England, is now a private house just up the road from the church. St Saviour's was built from 1901 to 1909 by the Earl of Derby to commemorate the safe return of his sons from the Boer War. He owned Crag Hall, which had been built in the early 19th century by George Palfreyman, the founder of the mill.

⊞ **FOREST CHAPEL:** This isolated hamlet comprising of a few buildings, which used to be the parsonage, school and pub, has

REFRESHMENTS:
THE CRAG INN, Wildboarclough. Open 12 noon to 3 pm and 7 pm to 11 pm (10.30 pm on Sunday). Telephone: 01260 227239.
THE STANLEY ARMS, Bottom of the Oven. Open 12 noon to 3 pm and 5.30 pm to 11 pm weekdays; 11 am to 11 pm on Saturday; 12 noon to 10.30 pm on Sunday. Telephone: 01260 252414.

long served this remote district. St Stephen's Chapel dates back to 1673 although it was rebuilt in 1834 and is one of the few places where the old Rush Bearing Ceremony is still held. In the days when churches were just open spaces and there were no pews for the congregation, there would be a covering of rushes or straw to absorb all the dirt on the floor. This was changed once a year, hence the ceremony, which at Forest Chapel happens on the first Sunday after the Glorious 12th August, when the Earl of Derby was likely to be in the area for the grouse shooting.

St. Stephen's Chapel

ASHFORD AND MONSAL HEAD

Length 5½ miles

With the placid waters of the Wye bustling with trout, the sweeping span of the old Sheep-wash Bridge framed by majestic trees, and the peaceful streets lined with rustic stone cottages, Ashford is reason enough on its own to merit this walk. Yet the drama ahead of you offers a distinct contrast to this gentle setting. The steeply sided Monsal Dale hemmed in by rich woodland, the stunning viewpoint from its head, and a walk over and under an 80 ft high railway viaduct are guaranteed to cause more than one sharp intake of breath! Add to this the beautiful settings created by the wind-ing river and its numerous weirs and falls, a ruined water mill, a woodland walk and you have one of the most memorable tours in the area – and wait till you see the pubs and cafés en route ...

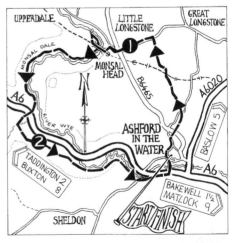

TERRAIN: One steep climb of about 150 ft near Deepdale, and a couple of shorter ones, but mainly good paths and only gentle

ascents. Paths at Monsal Head and near Deepdale can get slippery in wet weather.

GETTING THERE: From Buxton head south on
the A6 for about 9 miles and then turn left at
the signpost to Ashford Village. From Matlock
take the A6 north for about 9 miles and then
turn right at the A6020, and then left straight
after into the village. Parking is either at a small
car park up the lane behind the church or along
the roads in Ashford (be careful not to obstruct residents' access). NB: If parking is tight in Ashford you
could try Monsal Head's pay and display car parks (1¼
miles up the B6465) or the car park 2 miles up the A6
towards Buxton (where the walk crosses near point 2).

START: The walk starts from the small green at the top of
Fennel Street by the school. From here go up Vicarage Lane,
pass the farm at the top and then, just past the sign warn-
ing walkers that there is no footway, turn right through a gap
in the hedge and follow the signs to Monsal Head.

⊞ MONSAL TRAIL: Created after 1980 when the National Park
Authority purchased the section of the old London–Manchester
Midland railway from Bakewell to Wyedale and converted it into
an 8 mile long path (with diversions around the tunnels).
The line was originally built in the 1860s.

Ashford in the Water

Go through gap in wall and up path opposite to Ashford
DEEPDALE
2
To Taddington
Go up steps by Pay and display machine
Path goes right over open grass area to T-Junction. Go left up steep path to Ashford. At wall, go through gate and follow path which follows contour.
Toilets
A6
P
TAKE CARE CROSSING A6
To Brushfield
STREAM
Brushfield Hough
N
Settlement
Fin Cop
MONSAL DALE
RIVER WYE
Hob's House
Weir
Go right after Viaduct then right at bottom of path, along river and back under viaduct.
Posts
Monsal Head Viaduct
MONSAL HEAD
Toilets
Tunnel
Monsal View Cafe
MONSAL TRAIL
B6465
THE STABLES PUB
Monsal Head Hotel
TO UPPERDALE
Go through gap in wall and turn right down path. Turn left at next junction down path signposted to the Viaduct.
1
Chapel

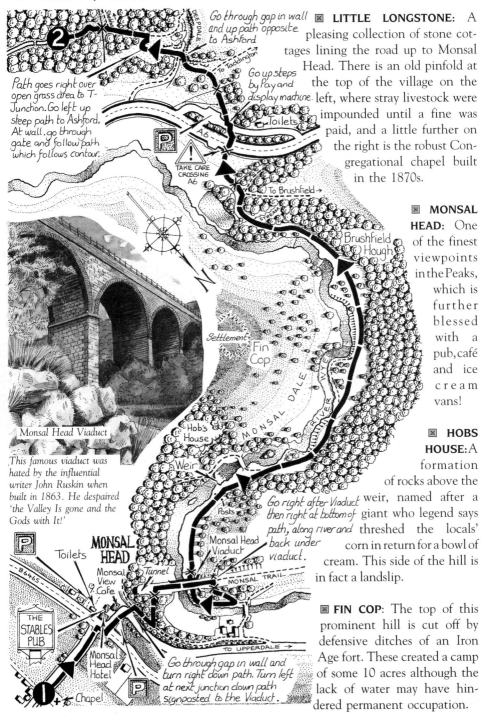

Monsal Head Viaduct

This famous viaduct was hated by the influential writer John Ruskin when built in 1863. He despaired 'the Valley Is gone and the Gods with It!'

LITTLE LONGSTONE: A pleasing collection of stone cottages lining the road up to Monsal Head. There is an old pinfold at the top of the village on the left, where stray livestock were impounded until a fine was paid, and a little further on the right is the robust Congregational chapel built in the 1870s.

MONSAL HEAD: One of the finest viewpoints in the Peaks, which is further blessed with a pub, café and ice cream vans!

HOBS HOUSE: A formation of rocks above the weir, named after a giant who legend says threshed the locals' corn in return for a bowl of cream. This side of the hill is in fact a landslip.

FIN COP: The top of this prominent hill is cut off by defensive ditches of an Iron Age fort. These created a camp of some 10 acres although the lack of water may have hindered permanent occupation.

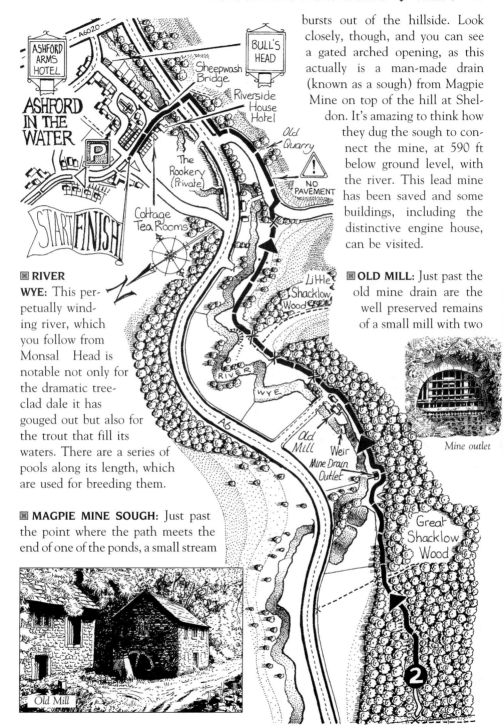

bursts out of the hillside. Look closely, though, and you can see a gated arched opening, as this actually is a man-made drain (known as a sough) from Magpie Mine on top of the hill at Sheldon. It's amazing to think how they dug the sough to connect the mine, at 590 ft below ground level, with the river. This lead mine has been saved and some buildings, including the distinctive engine house, can be visited.

⊠ **RIVER WYE:** This perpetually winding river, which you follow from Monsal Head is notable not only for the dramatic tree-clad dale it has gouged out but also for the trout that fill its waters. There are a series of pools along its length, which are used for breeding them.

⊠ **MAGPIE MINE SOUGH:** Just past the point where the path meets the end of one of the ponds, a small stream

⊠ **OLD MILL:** Just past the old mine drain are the well preserved remains of a small mill with two

Mine outlet

Old Mill

rusting water wheels at each end of the building. I believe that it was used to produce bobbins from ash and sycamore for the local cotton mills.

⌧ **BLACK MARBLE:** The area to the south of Ashford was famous for a small outcrop of black marble. It is, in fact, a thin, dark limestone, which, unlike most in the Peaks, was formed in deep water, and when polished came up satin black. It has been used from prehistoric times but especially in the 18th and 19th century for decorative pieces from memorials to fireplaces.

REFRESHMENTS:
THE PACKHORSE INN, Little Longstone. Welcoming pub for walkers and families. Open all day. Telephone: 01629 640471.
THE STABLES PUB (rear of the Monsal Head Hotel). Open all day. Telephone: 01629 640250.
MONSAL VIEW CAFE, Monsal Head. Open 10.30 am to 5 pm. Telephone: 01629 640346.
THE ASHFORD ARMS HOTEL, Church Street, Ashford in the Water. Open all day. Telephone: 01629 812725.
THE BULL'S HEAD, Church Street, Ashford in the Water. Open 11 am to 3 pm and 6 pm to 11 pm (12 noon to 3 pm on Sunday). Telephone: 01629 812931.

⌧ **ASHFORD IN THE WATER:** The most notable feature in this picturesque village is the old Sheepwash Bridge, originally a packhorse bridge, which was named after the small enclosure on its southern side where sheep were held while being washed in the waters of the Wye. Holy Trinity church contains some black marble memorials and is also famous for white paper garlands or 'Virgins' Crants', which were hung in the church after the funeral of an unmarried girl. They date from 1747 until 1801 when an Elizabeth Blackwell was found drowned in the river.

Monsal Dale

Walk 10
BEELEY AND CHATSWORTH
Length 3 miles

Park Cottage and Edensor

Set amidst tree-clad hills and astride the busy waters of the River Derwent, Chatsworth can have few equals among the nation's stately homes for grandeur within such a dramatic setting. Yet the glories of this most popular of country houses pour out of the confines of its stone exterior and into the countryside and villages around. Not many communities could claim to live in such an attractive pick and mix collection of architectural styles as the good folk of Edensor, while millers must have gazed with amazed and envious eyes at the estate water mill, a building fit for a Lord of the Manor! Unfortunately the owners' benevolence ran short when it came to pubs, so this gentle stroll through the park starts at Beeley to the south of the house.

TERRAIN: Generally flat. Most of the walk is over grass; can be muddy in a few places.

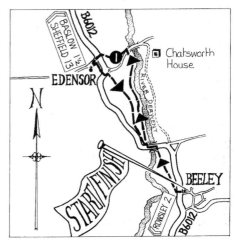

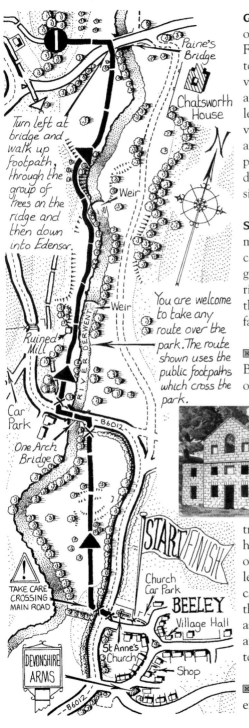

Paine's Bridge

Chatsworth House

N

Turn left at bridge and walk up footpath, through the group of trees on the ridge and then down into Edensor.

Weir

Ruined Mill

Weir

You are welcome to take any route over the park. The route shown uses the public footpaths which cross the park.

Car Park

One Arch Bridge

TAKE CARE CROSSING MAIN ROAD

Church Car Park

DEVONSHIRE ARMS

START/FINISH

BEELEY

Village Hall

St Anne's Church

Shop

B6012

GETTING THERE: Beeley is a mile south of the Chatsworth estate on the B6012. From Baslow head south past the entrance to Chatsworth, go over the bridge and the village is a mile on the left. From the A6 at Rowsley turn onto the B6012 and Beeley is 2 miles on your right. Parking in the village is limited to the roadside. Try and avoid stopping directly in front of residents' properties; it may be best to leave your car down one of the dead-end roads or alongside the church where the walk starts.

START: From the church cross over the main road (take care, especially of traffic coming round the bend to your left) and go into the field opposite. Turn to your right and head across the field, through the clusters of trees to the bridge in the far corner.

▨ **THE OLD MILL AND ONE ARCH BRIDGE:** Both of these structures at the south end of Chatsworth Park were built by Joseph Paine in 1759–60 while he was carrying out changes around the estate for the 4th Duke of Devonshire. The classically styled mill was working up to 1952, and was then damaged ten years later when two beech trees fell on it during a storm. The ruins have been preserved, including the remains of the wheel on the north side and the old leat running down to it from a sluice, which can still be seen on the riverbank just above the first weir. One Arch Bridge was built as part of the new road that was laid out at the time between Edensor and Beeley to keep the traffic out of sight of the house.

The Old Mill

▨ **CHATSWORTH HOUSE:** There was an existing, modest manor house in the area

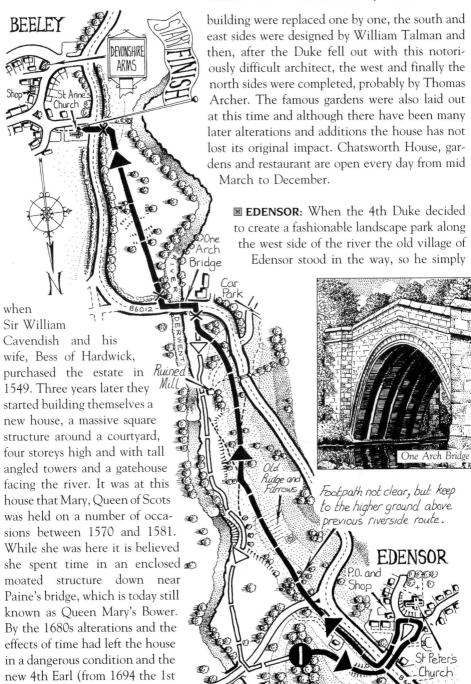

BEELEY

DEVONSHIRE ARMS

Shop
St Anne's Church

N

One Arch Bridge

Car Park

Ruined Mill

Old Ridge and Furrows

Footpath not clear, but keep to the higher ground above previous riverside route.

EDENSOR

P.O. and Shop

St Peter's Church

building were replaced one by one, the south and east sides were designed by William Talman and then, after the Duke fell out with this notoriously difficult architect, the west and finally the north sides were completed, probably by Thomas Archer. The famous gardens were also laid out at this time and although there have been many later alterations and additions the house has not lost its original impact. Chatsworth House, gardens and restaurant are open every day from mid March to December.

▣ **EDENSOR:** When the 4th Duke decided to create a fashionable landscape park along the west side of the river the old village of Edensor stood in the way, so he simply

when Sir William Cavendish and his wife, Bess of Hardwick, purchased the estate in 1549. Three years later they started building themselves a new house, a massive square structure around a courtyard, four storeys high and with tall angled towers and a gatehouse facing the river. It was at this house that Mary, Queen of Scots was held on a number of occasions between 1570 and 1581. While she was here it is believed she spent time in an enclosed moated structure down near Paine's bridge, which is today still known as Queen Mary's Bower. By the 1680s alterations and the effects of time had left the house in a dangerous condition and the new 4th Earl (from 1694 the 1st Duke) set about rebuilding it. The four sides of the original

One Arch Bridge

removed most of it out of sight. Even today as you return across the park from Edensor you can see humps and bumps in the grass, including lines of ridges and furrows, probably the remains of the village's medieval fields. Later again, in the 1830s, the 6th Duke completed the re-siting, all except for one stubborn resident who refused to move. His property, Park Cottage, still stands today, although it is also known as Naboth's Vineyard after the man who defied the king in the Bible. The new village was laid out to the north of the original by Joseph Paxton (who later built the Crystal Palace) from 1838–42, with the houses designed in part by John Robertson. The story goes that the 6th Duke was shown a catalogue of houses from which to choose a style for the village, but to the bemusement of the architect he asked for one of each design, resulting in the amazing array of houses which stand today. The village is dominated, though, by the overpowering spire of St Peter's church, which was rebuilt on the site of its medieval pre-

REFRESHMENTS:
THE DEVONSHIRE ARMS, Beeley. Open 11 am to 11 pm (12 noon to 10.30 pm on Sunday). Telephone: 01629 733259.
CARRIAGE HOUSE RESTAURANT, Chatsworth House. Open daily 10.15 am to 5.30 pm, mid March to December. Telephone: 01246 565300.

decessor in 1867 by Sir George Gilbert Scott. The churchyard contains the graves of Joseph Paxton and Kathleen Kennedy, the sister of President John Kennedy. She had married William, the eldest brother of the 11th Duke, in 1944 while in London with her father who was the American Ambassador. The couple had only five weeks together before William had to leave for the Continent where he died in active service a few months later. Kathleen passed away after a flying accident in France in 1948, and next to her grave is a plaque commemorating the visit her brother the President made in July 1963, only months before his own tragic death.

⊠**BEELEY:** Unlike Edensor, the village you see today is laid out to a medieval plan, although its Saxon name and the Bronze Age cairns on the moors above show that people had lived in the area for a long time before then. Beeley became absorbed into the Chatsworth estate after the previous owners, the Savilles, died out in 1734. Although Paxton built a number of houses here from 1838–41, much of what stands today is of an earlier date, giving the village a more authentic feel than its neighbour. St Anne's church, set amongst the trees at the highest point of the village, makes for an attractive start to the walk. Keep an eye out for a large single stone set in the wall on the south side of the church car park. This fills in a gap where a beehive used to stand.

Paine's bridge and Chatsworth House

Walk 11
DANEBRIDGE
Length 5 miles

The Hanging Stone

If variety is the spice of life then this tour through meadows, river gorges, a secret crevasse, wild moors and dramatic woodland should fulfil most appetites. The walk follows the remote River Dane as it winds through a valley flanked with sandstone cliffs and rich woodland, bereft of main roads and habitation, in which you stumble across hidden places oozing legend and mystery. The return route is across heather and tuft-covered grassland, with strange weathered stones appearing to thrust themselves out of the grassy slopes, before you plunge down through steep wooded slopes carved out by bubbling streams. The small hamlet of Danebridge with the picturesque Ship Inn welcomes the returning walker.

NB: Try and get to Danebridge early at weekends, as parking is limited.

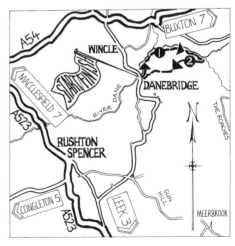

TERRAIN: One long, steady climb, generally good paths, a few damp patches.

GETTING THERE: From the south take the A523 north out of Leek and after 3 miles take the right turn signposted to Heaton and then at the top of the hill turn right again towards Swythamley. Follow this road for nearly 4 miles (watch out for the sharp bends) until you drop down into the Dane valley. Go across the bridge at the bottom and look to park along the roadside on the right. From the north take the A54 from either the Bosley crossroads or Buxton, and turn off at either turn to Wincle. Follow the road on to Danebridge, pass the Ship Inn and park at the bottom before the bridge.

START: From the roadside walk across the bridge, turn left over the stile and follow the footpath signposted to Gradbach.

▓**DANEBRIDGE:** Originally the road around which this hamlet has developed was a main route between Leek and Macclesfield and the crossing was known as Scliderford (slippery ford), a bit to the south of the present one. There was a bridge here by the 14th century; a twin-arched version was swept away by floods in 1631, while the present one was built as late as 1869. There are a few earlier houses but most date from the late 18th and 19th century when the mill, which had been hereabouts since at least the 1650s, was converted for cotton. It was in decline by the early 20th century and the building, which had stood behind the Methodist chapel (just below the start flag on the above map), was demolished in 1976.

▓**RIVER DANE:** This lesser known of Peak District rivers rises on Axe Edge above Buxton. The valley through which it is cut is underlined with millstone grit, a sandstone with quartz particles, whose hardness made

Danebridge

it ideal for millstones. All along this route you will notice the tiny bits of quartz and red sand on the paths, from the eroded grit. There are stories of a family who ate passers by in a cottage (now gone) by the bridge where the Black Brook joins.

Lud's Church

Turn right by signpost towards Swythamley, up steep path then turn right when you reach track and carry on up this more gentle gradient.

At T junction by rocks turn left and walk 200 yards and then turn right into narrow crevasse (Lud's church). Return by same path and resume previous route towards Swythamley

Follow path up right side of hedge beside farmhouse and down the other side (between fences). Enter wood beyond and follow right bank of river for about ¾ mile.

⊠ **LUD'S CHURCH:** This dramatic 60 ft deep crevasse was formed by a landslip as one side of the valley fell away from the other. It is assumed to have been named after Walter de Ludauk, who at the turn of the 15th century was a Lollard. These were followers of John Wycliffe, a 14th century radical philosopher who questioned aspects of the Church, but support for their beliefs became treasonable by 1414. Legend has it that Walter was leading a group in prayer in this secret crevasse when soldiers burst in and during the mêlée that followed, his daughter Alice was shot (this apparently happened in 1405, a bit early for the use of a gun!). She was buried at the entrance to Lud's Church while the others were taken to London. It is also believed that its haunting green cliffs were a location in the tale of *Sir Gawain and the Green Knight*.

◼ **HANGING STONE:** An eroded ledge of mill-stone grit that projects dramatically from the grass-covered hillside, giving excellent views from its top surface. The Brocklehurst family, owners of the nearby Swythamley Hall from 1832–1975, placed plaques firstly in memory of Burke (a pet dog who died in 1874) and then Lieutenant Colonel Courtney Brocklehurst who was killed on active service in Burma in 1942. Swythamley Hall, which can be seen from the stone, was originally a 13th century grange of Dieulacres Abbey (see Walk 16) although what stands today dates from the 17th to the 19th century, despite a serious fire in 1813.

> **REFRESHMENTS:**
> THE SHIP INN, Danebridge. A late 16th century inn up the hill to the north-west of the bridge. Open 12 noon to 3 pm (4 pm at weekends) and 7 pm to 11 pm. No food on Monday. Telephone: 01260 227217.
> TEAS: Served on summer weekends at the village chapel on the road back to Swythamley

View over Dane Valley

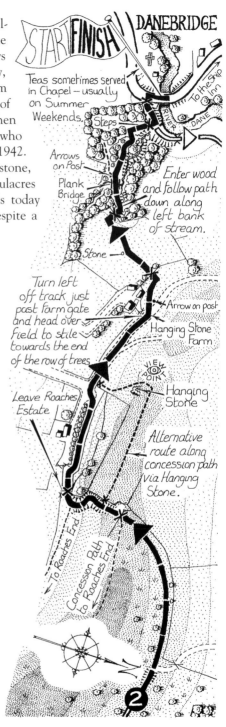

DANEBRIDGE

START FINISH

Teas sometimes served in Chapel – usually on Summer Weekends. Steps

To the Ship Inn

RIVER DANE

Arrows on Post

Plank Bridge

Enter wood and follow path down along left bank of stream.

Stone

Turn left off track just past farm gate and head over field to stile towards the end of the row of trees

Arrow on post

Hanging Stone Farm

VIEWPOINT

Leave Roaches Estate

Hanging Stone

Alternative route along concession path via Hanging Stone.

To Roaches End

Concession Path to Roaches End

2

Walk 12
LONGNOR
Length 4 miles

Longnor

Solid stone buildings and narrow back lanes welcome the visitor to this old market centre standing high on a ridge between the Dove and Manifold rivers. It retains the grandeur of a town, which it officially is, but has the charm of a village, which it resembles in size. Its numerous pubs and teashops act as a magnet for walkers starting out on routes exploring some of the most dramatic hills in the district, the most memorable being Parkhouse and Chrome Hills with their jagged limestone crests. This walk passes from Longnor across the ancient strip fields of the Dove valley and then around the bases of these imposing peaks. There are steep, rocky dales, a pub with the sign of a headless woman and numerous vantage points with commanding views of the countryside.

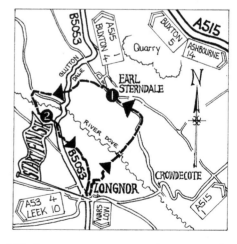

NB: Longnor can get very busy at weekends and in holiday periods so arrive as early as possible.

TERRAIN: One gentle climb spread over a mile and two short but steeper ascents (about 120 ft each). Some walking along minor roads. The return route is poorly marked in places and can be muddy.

GETTING THERE: Longnor is on the B5053 some 6 miles south of Buxton. Head out of Buxton on the A515 to Ashbourne and after 3 miles turn right onto the B5053, which takes you into Longnor. Parking (free) is on your left in the Market Place in the centre of the tiny town.

START: From the Market Place walk into the corner to the right of Longnor Craft Centre and up the lane alongside the Grapes Hotel. At the top turn left and then right almost straight away up a drive that leads to some garages. Just before these, turn right by the footpath sign and up a path leading out into the fields.

🔲 **THE DOVE VALLEY:** From the hill as you drop down into the valley of the fledgling Dove you will notice the long, strip-shaped fields that run from one side to the other, perpendicular to the river. These are probably the result of a piecemeal break up of medieval open fields, which has preserved the shape of the old narrow strips and was done long before the more ruthless enclosures of the late 18th and 19th centuries where the previous field patterns tended to get swept away. At the narrow Beggars Bridge there once stood a tannery, which attracted apprentices from Buxton and Leek.

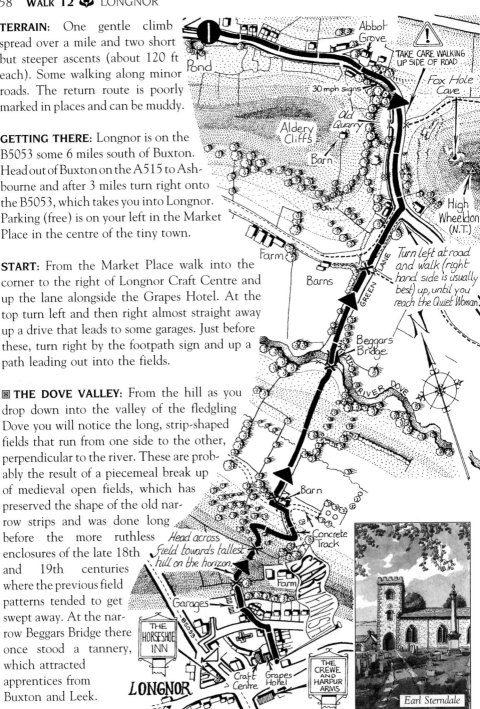

TAKE CARE WALKING UP SIDE OF ROAD

Fox Hole Cave

Abbot Grove

Pond

30 mph signs

Old Quarry

Aldery Cliffs

Barn

High Wheeldon (N.T.)

Farm

Barns

GREEN LANE

Turn left at road and walk (right hand side is usually best) up, until you reach the Quiet Woman.

Beggars Bridge

RIVER DOVE

Head across field towards tallest hill on the horizon.

Barn

Concrete Track

Farm

Garages

THE HORSESHOE INN

LONGNOR

Craft Centre

Grapes Hotel

THE CREWE AND HARPUR ARMS

Earl Sterndale

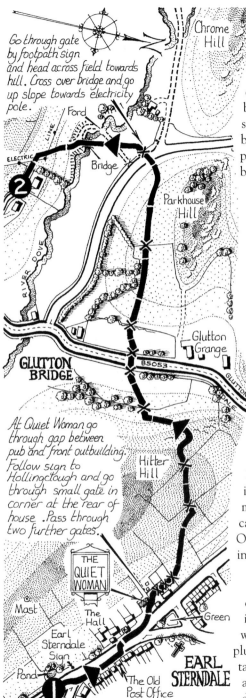

Go through gate
by footpath sign
and head across field towards
hill. Cross over bridge and go
up slope towards electricity
pole.

Ford

ELECTRIC LINE

Bridge

2

RIVER DOVE

Parkhouse
Hill

Chrome
Hill

Glutton
Grange

GLUTTON
BRIDGE

B5053

GLUTTON DALE

At Quiet Woman go
through gap between
pub and front outbuilding.
Follow sign to
Hollingclough and go
through small gate in
corner at the rear of
house. Pass through
two further gates.

Hitter
Hill

THE
QUIET
WOMAN

Mast

The
Hall

Earl
Sterndale
Sign

Pond

The Old
Post Office

Green

EARL
STERNDALE

▦ HIGH WHEELDON AND FOX HOLE
CAVE: This hill, which rises to 1,384 ft, was given to the National Trust in 1946 in memory of those lost in World War II from Derbyshire and Staffordshire, the border of which runs along the River Dove below. Fox Hole Cave has been a source of some of the earliest human finds in the Peaks but its tiny entrance is barred in order to preserve them. (You can walk up the hill but it is very steep.)

Parkhouse and Chrome Hills

▦ EARL STERNDALE: This scattering of
farms and cottages, which reaches a pleasant crescendo around its green, is of some antiquity. Its church, although rebuilt in 1952 after a stray German bomb damaged it during the war, stands on the site of a medieval chapel and still retains a crudely carved font that could be over 900 years old. Opposite is the Quiet Woman, with a painting of a headless woman on its sign. This apparently represents the nagging wife of a former landlord who lost his cool and chopped her head off. Rather than berating the crime, the locals had a whip round, which paid for the headstone and left surplus money for the murdering publican. So take heed of the saying 'soft words turneth away wrath' before entering into a heated debate in this 400 year old hostelry!

⊠ **PARKHOUSE AND CHROME HILLS:** These impressive jagged limestone hills were reefs (a build up of mud and seaweed), which formed as a fringe between deep water (on their southern slopes) and a lagoon (on their northern) in a tropical sea more than 300 million years ago.

⊠ **LONGNOR:** First mentioned in 1223, Longnor (meaning Long Ridge) was from early on an important centre for trade in the area. The markets prospered from the medieval period, peaking in the 19th century when Sir John Harpur Crewe built the present Market House (note the tolls on the panel above the door dating from 1903). In the churchyard (where the earliest markets were held) stands the imposing St Bartholomew's church of 1780, while on the main road is the impressively fronted Wesleyan church of 1855, both buildings of a size that would grace a vastly larger town. The attractive narrow back lanes are flanked by stone buildings, which mostly date from the 18th and 19th centuries.

REFRESHMENTS:
THE CREWE AND HARPUR ARMS, Market Square, Longnor. Good views from the garden. Open 12 noon to 2 pm and 5 pm to 11 pm; all day on Saturday and Sunday. Telephone: 01298 83205.
THE HORSESHOE INN, Longnor. Welcoming pub serving light snacks all day. Open 11 am to 11 pm; 12 noon to 10.30 pm on Sunday. Telephone: 01298 83262.
THE QUIET WOMAN, Earl Sterndale. Genuine village local, worth a stop en route. Open 11 am to 3 pm and 7 pm to 11 pm; 12 noon to 3 pm on Sunday. Telephone: 01298 83211.
LONGNOR CRAFT CENTRE AND COFFEE SHOP, Longnor. Open 10 am to 5 pm daily from March to December; Friday to Sunday in January and February, 10 am to 5 pm. Telephone: 01298 83587.
MANIFOLD TEA ROOMS, Longnor. Open 9 am to 5 pm on Saturday and Sunday, also 10 am to 4 pm on Thursday and Friday in summer.

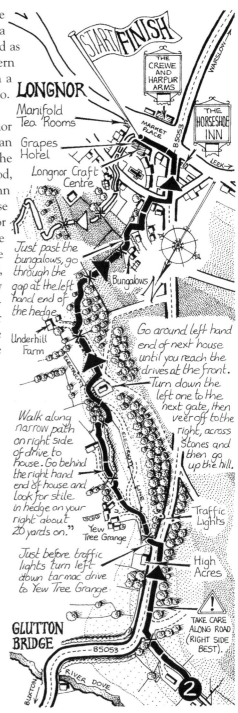

Walk 13
YOULGREAVE
Length 4½ miles

Alport

A *gentle walk through a dale of delights! From a deep wooded valley broken by outcrops of rock reflecting in a string of tranquil pools, down to open fields with the River Bradford meandering under limestone cliffs, this constantly changing landscape is complemented by three of the finest Peak District villages. Middleton with its stone cottages shaded under mighty trees, Alport's rustic houses creating the idyllic riverside setting, and Youlgreave, an amazing collection of buildings straddling a ridge, dominated by the huge Perpendicular church tower. Add to this old mine shafts, clapper bridges, ruined mills and a fine collection of pubs and you have a walk you will find hard to resist.*

NB: You could do a shorter walk by simply missing the loop to Middleton.

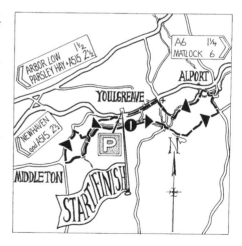

TERRAIN: A few gentle climbs and some narrow paths but generally good underfoot.

Clapper Bridge

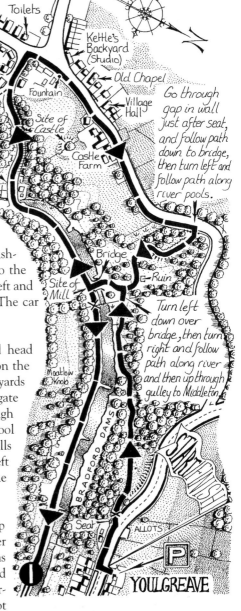

MIDDLETON
Toilets
Kettle's
Backyard
(Studio)
Old Chapel
Farm
Fountain
Village
Hall
Site of
Castle
Ruins of old
factory
Castle
Farm
RIVER BRADFORD
Bridge
Ruin
Site of
Mill
Moatlow
Knob
BRADFORD DAMS
Seat
ALLOTS
P
YOULGREAVE

Go through
gap in wall
just after seat,
and follow path
down to bridge,
then turn left and
follow path along
river pools.

Turn left
down over
bridge, then turn
right and follow
path along river
and then up through
gulley to Middleton.

GETTING THERE: Youlgreave is 3 miles south of Bakewell. From here take the A6 towards Matlock and then turn right just past Haddon Hall down the B5056. Take the first right and continue through Alport, and on through Youlgreave until you reach the car park at the far end of the village. From the west use the A515 Buxton to Ashbourne road and turn off at Newhaven onto the A5012, and then almost straight away turn left and follow this road for 4 miles to Youlgreave. The car park is on the left as you enter the village.

START: From the car park turn right and head away from the village along the pavement on the left side of the road. After a few hundred yards turn off onto the footpath by the seat and gate on your left, and follow the path down through the trees and then along the edge of the pool at the bottom. After passing over two walls you come to a T-junction where you turn left down to the bridge, and then go right on the other side.

▩ **MIDDLETON:** In the dale as you walk up to the village there is a large boulder under the cliff, known as Fulwood's Rock. This was the last hiding place of Christopher Fulwood who, after raising an army for the King during the Civil War, was caught at this spot just below his home and was then shot by the Parliamentarians. His house, known as Fulwood's Castle, has long since gone although there are remains at the rear of Castle Farm of what was probably a fortified house rather than a military stronghold. Another notable local was Thomas Bateman (1821–1861) of Lomberdale Hall (a Gothic man-

Old Mill

ALPORT

RIVER LATHKILL

Monks Hall

Go through gap on corner of road and follow path down to river.

Millfield Farm

Rhienstor Plantation

Site of Blyth Mines

Old Co-op

Cross over small bridge by the seat under rock and go up path

GEORGE HOTEL

BRADFORD

All Saints' Church

BRASSINGTON CLOSE

RIVER BRADFORD

Old Mine Shafts

Seat under rock

Hollow Farm

Braemar Hs.

EAST VIEW

CONKSBURY LANE

ROAD NARROWS

Conduit Head

Thimble Hall

BAINES LN.

CHURCH ST.

MAIN ST.

MOOR LN.

BULL'S HEAD

Old Co Op (YHA)

YOULGREAVE

Go up track to Hollow Farm

Clapper Bridge

THE FARMYARD INN

HOLYWELL LANE

Clapper Bridge

GROVE PLACE

GRIMBLES LN.

Chapel

COLDWELL END

Tearooms

KING ST.

P

STARV FINISH

sion of 1845 halfway between here and Youlgreave) who dug up nearly 400 ancient barrows across the Peaks in search of treasure! He is buried in a railed tomb at the rear of the old Congregational chapel (1826) on the left side of the road, just past the fountain. Today this hardy estate village, still with working farms amongst the surrounding stone cottages and houses, makes a picturesque scene under the canopy of trees.

⊠ **MIDDLETON HALL:** This house at the west end of the village was rebuilt in 1824–7 for Thomas Bateman's father, before the family moved to Lomberdale Hall.

⊠ **LEAD MINING:** Although placid today, the hills above Bradford Dale were riddled with mines and spoil heaps in the 18th century. A number of the old shafts can be seen just above Hollow Farm. On the side of the hill to the south-west of here stood Mawstone Mine

All Saints' Church

where the worst accident in Derbyshire lead mining happened when eight men were killed in an explosion caused by firedamp (a combustible gas).

⌗ **ALPORT:** This ancient riverside hamlet stood where the old Portway and a later packhorse route forded the river. It wasn't until after a report in 1718 complaining at the state of the crossing that a horse bridge was built, the current one replacing it some time later. The corn mill just downstream of here dates from the 18th century and a bit further down is a later lead smelting works. (The Bradford dams were built to store up water for Alport's lead mill although today they are used for breeding trout.) Water supply has been a problem in the past as the River Bradford vanished underground for a time in the 19th century due to flooding and mining opening up a new route downstream, until it cured itself. A more notable subterranean route

was the sough (mine drainage tunnel) stretching from the Duke of Rutland's Alport mines to the River Derwent some 4½ miles away. It was the longest in the county and while it was being built (1766–87) was the site of one of the first recorded strikes when a 7-day working week was forced on the miners to speed up construction. Alport stood in an intense mining area in the 17th and 18th centuries and its pleasant stone buildings reflect the wealth of the times, while Monk's Hall just behind the junction of the Lathkill and Bradford dates from the late 1500s (the little bridge you cross at the bottom of the hill as you enter Alport was originally a private entrance to this house).

⌗ **YOULGREAVE:** A proud and independent hilltop settlement, spelt 'Youlgrave' by locals but known better as 'Pommie' by the villagers (possibly a reference to the noise made by its old silver band). Few places in England still have their own private water supply, piped off the gritstone moors to the south since 1829 when the old conduit head (a stone water tank of 1,500 gallons capacity) was built opposite the Bull's Head. The range of buildings, which straddle the ridge, is diverse, from the distinguished Old Hall of the 1650s to the imposing Victorian Co-op stores, which seems to have been plucked out of a town and placed amidst the humble cottages! Opposite here is the tiny Thimble Hall, its couple of rooms overlooking the old conduit head, while at the other end of the spectrum is the huge All Saints' church with its tower nearly 100 ft high, dominating the landscape around. In medieval times All Saints' church was at the centre of a large parish so that villagers from as far as Winster, Elton, Stanton and Middleton had to come to Youlgreave for weddings and funerals. Much of the church you see today would have been familiar to them, from the round, stout piers inside the nave dating from the late 12th century to the Perpendicular tower of the late 1400s. The notable Norman font with its odd second bowl supported by a carved salamander (a symbol of baptism), however, would not have been, as it was originally at Elton and only came here via the vicar's garden when their church was being rebuilt in the early 19th century. When they offered Youlgreave £5 to make a new one so they could have the original back, their larger neighbour stood firm and it was Elton that had to make do with the replica. Just outside the church porch is a square set of steps with a bottle-shaped block of masonry on top. The steps are the base of the old market cross, which originally stood opposite the Bull's Head but was moved here when

the conduit head was erected in 1829, while the piece on top is an upturned font reused to hold a sundial.

REFRESHMENTS:

THE BULL'S HEAD, Fountain Square, Youlgreave. Open 11 am to 3 pm and 6 pm to 11 pm (12 noon to 3 pm and 7 pm to 10.30 pm on Sunday). Telephone: 01629 636307.

THE FARMYARD INN, Main Street, Youlgreave. Open 11.30 am to 3 pm and 7 pm to 11 pm (12 noon to 3 pm and 7 pm to 10.30 pm on Sunday). Small beer garden to the side. Telephone: 01629 636221.

THE GEORGE HOTEL, Church Street, Youlgreave. Open all day, 11 am to 11 pm (12 noon to 10.30 pm on Sunday). Telephone: 01629 636292.

MEADOW COTTAGE TEAROOMS, Holywell Lane, Youlgreave. Telephone: 01629 636523. Open weekends and bank holidays and daily during the school summer holiday. Still has 'Teas with Hovis' sign outside!

The bridge and seat under the rock at the bottom of Braemar Lane.

Walk 14
THE ROACHES
Length 4 miles

Hen Cloud

*T*he gateway into the Peak District from the south-west is memorably marked by an immense wall of millstone grit known as the Roaches. These rippling crags have many moods, casting a sombre grey outline against an overcast sky or glowing violent red in the setting sun. The sheer rock face is in dramatic contrast to its passive reverse side, a wild and often overlooked tract of moorland, with small farmsteads cut out of the rough grass making a patchwork of subtle colours across this sweeping landscape. This walk encompasses both of these aspects as you travel past isolated gritstone houses, along streams and through heather, to return with stunning views over Staffordshire.

NB: Although the Roaches are now open to roam, please keep to paths and respect warnings of grouse shoots. Alternative routes are marked.

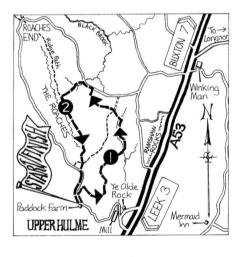

TERRAIN: Very boggy in places – walking boots a must! One notable but steady climb, with two steep descents (one a flight of steps).

GETTING THERE: The Roaches are just off the A53 between Buxton and Leek. From either direction turn off at the sign to Upper Hulme and then turn left if coming from the south or right if coming from the north, down the narrow lane, round past the old mill, and then up to run along the base of the hills. Park in the lay-by opposite the Roaches Tearooms (there are other lay-bys further on). Note that the parking spaces can fill very quickly on sunny weekends, so arrive early or alternatively use the park and ride service from Tittesworth Reservoir.

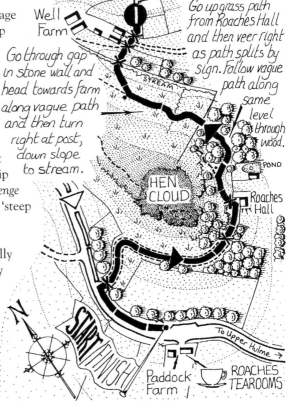

Roaches Hall

START: From the lay-by carry on along the road away from the direction you came, and then turn right and go up the track signposted to Roaches Hall.

⊞ **UPPER HULME:** The small village you travel through on your way up to the Roaches probably gets its name from the Norse word *holmr*, meaning 'raised ground in marshy land', which is quite appropriate as you will soon find out!

⊞ **HEN CLOUD:** This dramatic outcrop of sandstone stands alone at 1,350 ft and marks the southern tip of the Roaches. Its name was *Henge Clud*, which in Old English means 'steep hill'.

⊞ **ROACHES HALL:** This dramatically located private house was originally called Argyle Cottage when it was built in 1876.

⊞ **THE BLUE HILLS AND GOLD-SITCH MOSS:** The open tract of moorland covered by the second strip map is flanked on the east by the Blue Hills and

Well Farm

Go through gap in stone wall and head towards farm along vague path and then turn right at post, down slope to stream.

Go up grass path from Roaches Hall and then veer right as path splits by sign. Follow vague path along same level through wood.

STREAM

POND

HEN CLOUD

Roaches Hall

START/FINISH

N

To Upper Hulme →

Paddock Farm

ROACHES TEAROOMS

to the north by Goldsitch Moss (named after the marigolds that grow along Black Brook). This now tranquil land was until the early 20th century the home of coal miners, who worked small, scattered pits producing a limited quantity of fuel, probably for the burning of limestone in the Buxton area. There are records of this little industry from as early as the 16th century, and by the 19th a number of shafts and around six colliers were established in the area behind Shaw Cottage (disused by

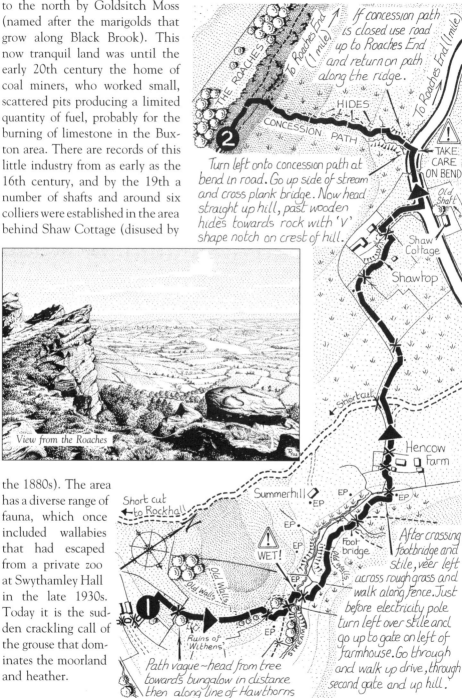

If concession path is closed use road up to Roaches End and return on path along the ridge.

Turn left onto concession path at bend in road. Go up side of stream and cross plank bridge. Now head straight up hill, past wooden hides towards rock with 'V' shape notch on crest of hill.

View from the Roaches

the 1880s). The area has a diverse range of fauna, which once included wallabies that had escaped from a private zoo at Swythamley Hall in the late 1930s. Today it is the sudden crackling call of the grouse that dominates the moorland and heather.

After crossing footbridge and stile, veer left across rough grass and walk along fence. Just before electricity pole turn left over stile and go up to gate on left of farmhouse. Go through and walk up drive, through second gate and up hill.

Path vague ~ head from tree towards bungalow in distance then along line of Hawthorns

Rockhall

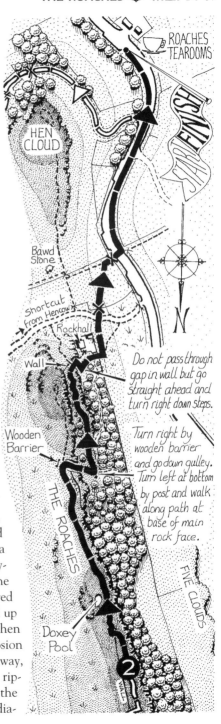

ROACHES TEAROOMS

HEN CLOUD

START/FINISH

Bawd Stone

Shortcut from Hencow

Rockhall

Wall

Wooden Barrier

THE ROACHES

Doxey Pool

FIVE CLOUDS

Do not pass through gap in wall but go straight ahead and turn right down steps.

Turn right by wooden barrier and go down gulley. Turn left at bottom by post and walk along path at base of main rock face.

THE ROACHES: This strange name is derived from *roche*, a French word meaning rock or cliff, and is recorded as such from at least 1358. The Roaches themselves date back a little further, 300 million years roughly speaking, when this part of the country was a delta somewhere near the equator. Grains of minerals were swept down the river from a mountain range where Scotland now stands and became cemented over time to form bands of a sandstone known as millstone grit between layers of mud, shale and coal, depending upon the height and conditions of the sea, which bordered this area. Over the ages these rocks were lifted up and folded (creating a ripple effect) and were then buried under nearly 2 miles of later rock. Erosion from rivers, wind and rain has worn these all away, leaving today the bottom half of one of these ripples of sandstone exposed – its western side is the Roaches and its east is Ramshaw Rocks (see dia-

300–290 million years ago.	290–65 million years ago.	65 million – 10,000 years ago.	10,000 years ago ~ Today.
River from Scotland	Later Deposits	Erosion	ROACHES / RAMSHAW ROCKS
Sea / Delta	Folding	Sandstone	Shale Sandstone / BROOK
Mud, Shale and Coal / Sandstone	Mud, Shale and Coal		Peat formed but now eroding.
Limestone	Uplift		

gram). The Roaches with its summit of 1,658 ft was purchased by the Peak Park Board in 1980.

❖ **ROCKHALL:** A mid 19th century Gothic style hunting lodge built over the front of a cave, which had been inhabited and known as Rockhall from at least 1770. After years of being a private home it was opened as a retreat for mountaineers in 1993.

REFRESHMENTS:
THE ROACHES TEAROOMS, Paddocks Farm, Upper Hulme. Open from March to November, 9 am to 5.30 pm daily (except Tuesday). Good range of food including Staffordshire Oatcakes (a must for the hungry walker!). Telephone: 01538 300345.
YE OLDE ROCK INN, Upper Hulme. Large pub with excellent range of food and beers. Telephone: 01538 300324.

View to Hen Cloud

Walk 15
WINSTER AND
STANTON MOOR
Length 5½ miles

Winster Market Hall

It's hard to imagine that the quiet, rambling roads of Winster or the wild, heather clad Stanton Moor have ever been touched by the hands of industry, yet this whole south-eastern segment of the Peak District was once a thriving lead mining and quarrying area. What you see on this walk today, though, is a reminder of how time and nature wear down and reclaim even the most scarred landscapes. Winster is a fascinating maze of narrow, winding back lanes and large rustic stone houses with the only visible record of mining lying as grassed over humps and bumps in the surrounding fields. Man's touch has been more sympathetic in other places – such as the amazing caves and sculptured features on Rowter Rocks or the prehistoric Nine Ladies Stone Circle.

NB: There are numerous paths across Stanton Moor, which you are free to explore.

The route chosen keeps to the public footpaths and passes most of the prehistoric features.

TERRAIN: There are two short climbs of about 200 ft and a number of smaller ones. The route can be muddy to the north of Winster even in summer.

GETTING THERE: From the south or west use the A5012 between Newhaven (on the A515) and Cromford, and turn off onto the B5056 to Winster at Grangemill. After 1½ miles turn right opposite the Miners Standard and the car park for Winster is immediately on your right. From the north take the A6, and 2 miles south of Bakewell turn off on the B5056. Follow this road for 4 miles and then turn left at the top of the hill by the Miners Standard and into the car park.

START: From the car park start down towards Winster but take the first right, East Bank, along the top of the hill. After the open common area turn left down the lane opposite Pinfold Cottage, walk past the chapel and at the bottom of the steps turn left and then right. This lane

Go over right hand stile and walk up hill, through 2 gates and Stoop Wood, then walk along left side of fence at the top.

Dower House gateposts

Dower House

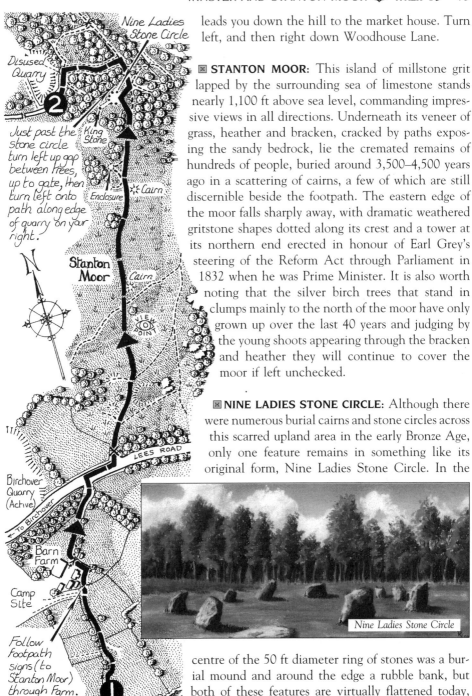

Nine Ladies
Stone Circle

Disused
Quarry

Just past the
stone circle
turn left up gap
between trees,
up to gate, then
turn left onto
path along edge
of quarry on your
right.

King
Stone

Enclosure   ⁚: Cairn

N

Stanton
Moor   Cairn

VIEW
POINT

LEES ROAD

Birchover
Quarry
(Active)

Barn
Farm

Camp
Site

Follow
footpath
signs (to
Stanton Moor)
through Farm.

leads you down the hill to the market house. Turn left, and then right down Woodhouse Lane.

⊠ **STANTON MOOR:** This island of millstone grit lapped by the surrounding sea of limestone stands nearly 1,100 ft above sea level, commanding impressive views in all directions. Underneath its veneer of grass, heather and bracken, cracked by paths exposing the sandy bedrock, lie the cremated remains of hundreds of people, buried around 3,500–4,500 years ago in a scattering of cairns, a few of which are still discernible beside the footpath. The eastern edge of the moor falls sharply away, with dramatic weathered gritstone shapes dotted along its crest and a tower at its northern end erected in honour of Earl Grey's steering of the Reform Act through Parliament in 1832 when he was Prime Minister. It is also worth noting that the silver birch trees that stand in clumps mainly to the north of the moor have only grown up over the last 40 years and judging by the young shoots appearing through the bracken and heather they will continue to cover the moor if left unchecked.

⊠ **NINE LADIES STONE CIRCLE:** Although there were numerous burial cairns and stone circles across this scarred upland area in the early Bronze Age, only one feature remains in something like its original form, Nine Ladies Stone Circle. In the

Nine Ladies Stone Circle

centre of the 50 ft diameter ring of stones was a burial mound and around the edge a rubble bank, but both of these features are virtually flattened today, while just to the south-west is the King Stone. The strange name is said to come from nine ladies who were turned to stone for dancing on the Sabbath, while the fiddler who played the music is now the lonely King Stone.

❋ **BIRCHOVER:** A village strung out along a main street, which has grown up over the past 300 years mainly to house workers from the nearby quarries. The use of this local building stone and the apparently haphazard arrangement of the houses adds great charm, complemented by the old chapels and pubs.

❋ **ROWTER ROCKS:** Just behind the Druid Inn is a small outcrop of millstone grit called Rowter Rocks. As the name of the pub implies there are tales of ancient religious activities and magic being performed upon these strange weathered stones and yet it was a religious man of more recent origin who was responsible for the real magic of this lofty spot. The Rev Thomas Eyre, who built

Go back to first map and work down the page from point ③.

Rowter Rocks

Just past quarry works turn right into car park (by footpath sign). Go straight across gravel area and follow path between two sculptured stones.

Route a bit vague in places! As you enter wooded area and just past the second of two low stones, turn left. This path becomes more clear as you go round the top of the old quarry.

the first chapel (now the village church) below the rocks, spent much time entertaining friends and writing up sermons here and set about carving seats and caves in the rocks. Today you can walk up and explore these via the path behind the Druid Inn.

Rowter Rocks

UPPERTOWN: A tiny hamlet on the quiet road back to Winster, with a set of stocks in front of Uppertown Farm, restored in 1951.

WINSTER: The grand stone houses and narrow winding back lanes (ginnels or jitties), which make what was once one of the largest towns in Derbyshire such a delight to the eye today, are a reflection of the money that was made and the unplanned way in which the town expanded during the 18th century boom in lead mining. Lead metal is found in the mineral galena, which crystallised in veins when hot liquids were forced up through the surrounding limestone 180–270 million years ago. Miners dug shafts into the long, vertical faults called rakes (and the smaller veins off these called scrins) but were limited by technology and flooding. Investment in the mines around Winster by consortiums like the London Lead Co in the early 1700s and the arrival of the

REFRESHMENTS:
THE DRUID INN, Birchover. Open 12 noon to 2 pm and 7 pm to 11 pm (10.30 pm on Sunday). Excellent food – worth phoning ahead to book a seat. Telephone: 01629 650302.
THE RED LION, Birchover. A walker friendly pub with a glass covered well! Open 12 noon to 2 pm and 7 pm to 11 pm (11 am to 11 pm on Saturday in summer); Sunday 12 noon to 10.30 pm. Telephone: 01629 650363.
THE OLD BOWLING GREEN, East Bank, Winster. Open 6 pm to 11 pm during the week; 11 am to 11 pm on Saturday and 12 noon to 10.30 pm on Sunday. Telephone: 01629 650219.
THE MINERS STANDARD, Bank Top (on B5056 just across from the car park), Winster. Named after the standard dish that miners used to measure their ore. Open 12 noon to 4 pm and 6.30 pm to 11 pm (10.30 pm on Sunday). Telephone: 01629 650279.

first steam pumping engines (Yatestoop Mine 1719, just south-east of Stoop Wood) fuelled the expansion of the town. The market house, which originally had open arches below dating from the 16th century, had a new brick upper storey built around this time, although this was rebuilt in 1905 shortly before the National Trust acquired the building. There are many other impressive buildings along the main street although the twin gabled Dower House of 17th century origin and with wonderfully carved gateposts is particularly notable, standing as it does at the head of the road. By the 19th century the increasing costs of pumping and the falling price of lead resulted in the closure of the mines, with some miners transferring to local quarries and others leaving the district altogether. Winster is also noteworthy for the many traditional customs associated with it, including the Wakes at the end of June, the Guisers who perform mummers' plays at Christmas and the Morris Dancers who have appeared as far away as Lithuania.

Cork Stone

The Cork Stone above was so named after its resemblance to the cork of a bottle. Quarrymen have put rungs up one side to climb it!

Walk 16
LEEK AND RUDYARD LAKE
Length 5½ miles

St Edward's Church and Clerk Bank, Leek

*E*mbracing the south-western edge of the Peak District are the windswept moors and rocky outcrops of the Staffordshire Moorlands. High on a sandstone ridge at their centre stands the Victorian mill town of Leek, which has remarkably retained much of its quality building from this period when it prospered with the arrival of the canal and railway. Both of these made use of the nearby Rudyard Lake, the former built it as a water supply, the other took advantage of the dramatic tree-clad setting to attract tourists along its line. This walk follows both the old railway and canal feeder in a round trip to the tranquil lake squeezed within the steeply wooded valley and returns via the hidden ancient parts of Leek.

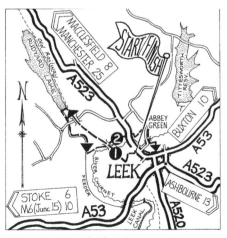

TERRAIN: Mostly flat, but two short, steep climbs on the return into Leek.

GETTING THERE: From Leek town centre take the A523 towards Macclesfield down the long hill past the Big Mill on your left, and at the bottom turn right by the sign to Meerbrook (Abbey Green Road) and there is parking alongside the road up to the 30 mph signs.

START: The walk starts from outside Brindley Mill back on Macclesfield Road. Cross over the road and go up Kiln Lane, which runs up the left side of the Dyers Arms. Carry on over the top of the hill and down the other side. Just before the railway bridge turn left along the footpath and then right down the steps onto the old railway line. Turn right under the bridge and continue to Rudyard.

▣ **BRINDLEY MILL:** There has almost certainly been a mill on this site since medieval times, long before James Brindley, a young millwright who had served his apprenticeship locally, designed the current building in the 1750s. He went on to become one of the leading canal engineers, the father of the waterways, while his humble water mill became rather dwarfed by later factories and fell into disuse in the 1940s. Thanks to local conservationists it was saved and returned to working order in 1974 and is open from 2 pm to 4 pm most Sundays through the summer and on bank holidays.

▣ **CHURNET VALLEY RAILWAY:** In the euphoria of the early railway mania there were many grand schemes vying with each other to achieve the shortest route, in this case from Manchester to London. The Churnet Valley line was a toned down version of one such scheme; a double track line opened in 1849 with stations at Leek and Rudyard a year later. Since the line closed in the 1960s its route in this area

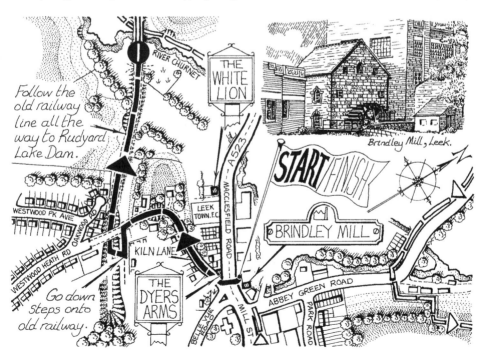

Follow the old railway line all the way to Rudyard Lake Dam.

Go down steps onto old railway.

Brindley Mill, Leek.

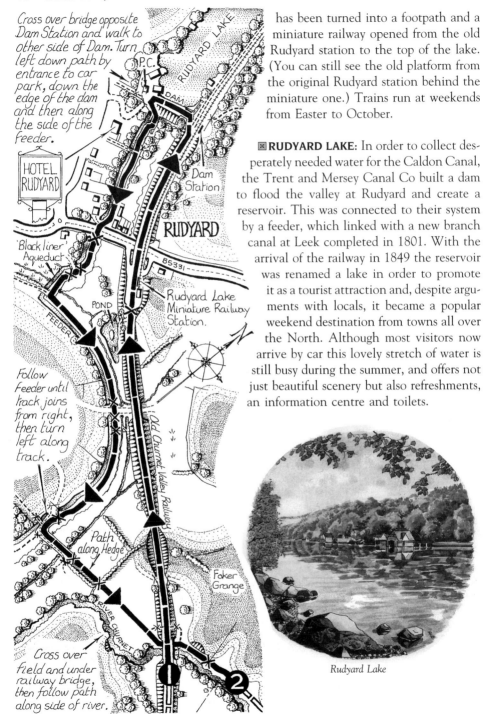

Cross over bridge opposite Dam Station and walk to other side of Dam. Turn left down path by entrance to car park, down the edge of the dam and then along the side of the feeder.

HOTEL RUDYARD

'Black liner' Aqueduct

POND

Dam Station

RUDYARD

B5331

Rudyard Lake Miniature Railway Station.

Follow feeder until track joins from right, then turn left along track.

Path along Hedge

Foker Grange

Cross over field and under railway bridge, then follow path along side of river.

RUDYARD LAKE

FEEDER

Old Churnet Valley Railway

RIVER CHURNET

has been turned into a footpath and a miniature railway opened from the old Rudyard station to the top of the lake. (You can still see the old platform from the original Rudyard station behind the miniature one.) Trains run at weekends from Easter to October.

⊠ **RUDYARD LAKE:** In order to collect desperately needed water for the Caldon Canal, the Trent and Mersey Canal Co built a dam to flood the valley at Rudyard and create a reservoir. This was connected to their system by a feeder, which linked with a new branch canal at Leek completed in 1801. With the arrival of the railway in 1849 the reservoir was renamed a lake in order to promote it as a tourist attraction and, despite arguments with locals, it became a popular weekend destination from towns all over the North. Although most visitors now arrive by car this lovely stretch of water is still busy during the summer, and offers not just beautiful scenery but also refreshments, an information centre and toilets.

Rudyard Lake

■ **DIEULACRES ABBEY:** The Cistercian monks of Poulton in Cheshire relocated in 1214 to a new site just to the north of Leek, probably because they were being hounded by Welsh raiders. Legend, though, says that their patron, the Earl of Chester, had a dream in which he was instructed by his grandfather, the patron of the original Poulton Abbey, to relocate his foundation, handily also telling his grandson when and where to site it. When the Earl awoke and told his wife, the Countess declared 'Deux encres!', whereupon he decided that the new abbey would be called 'Dieulacres'. The monks set about adapting their new site, which included moving the River Churnet up against the far side of the valley to create space in the valley for agriculture (the earthwork bank which retains its waters today is probably still the one that the

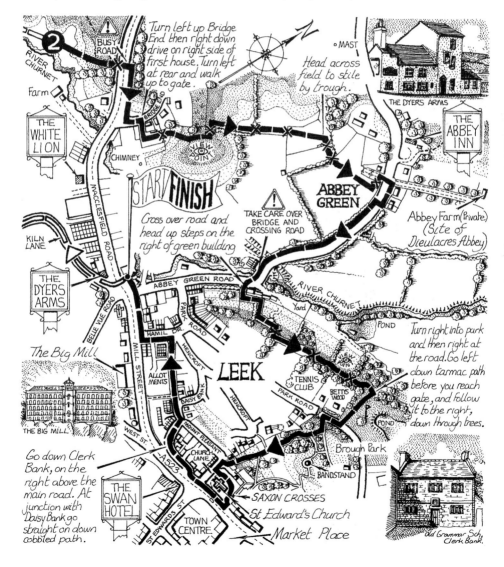

Turn left up Bridge End then right down drive on right side of first house. Turn left at rear and walk up to gate.

Head across field to stile by trough.

o MAST

THE DYERS ARMS

RIVER CHURNET

Farm

THE WHITE LION

CHIMNEY

BRIDGE END

VIEW POINT

START/FINISH

Cross over road and head up steps on the right of green building

TAKE CARE OVER BRIDGE AND CROSSING ROAD

ABBEY GREEN

THE ABBEY INN

Abbey Farm (Private) (Site of Dieulacres Abbey)

KILN LANE

MACCLESFIELD ROAD

THE DYERS ARMS

BELLE VUE ROAD

MILL STREET

ABBEY GREEN ROAD

PARK ROAD

HAMIL DR

HENCROFT

RIVER CHURNET

Yard

POND

The Big Mill

THE BIG MILL

ALLOTMENTS

DAISY BANK

WEST ST.

DAISY BANK

MOUNT PLEASANT

LEEK

HENCROFT

PARK ROAD

TENNIS CLUB

BETTS WOOD

NEW POND

Turn right into park and then right at the road. Go left down tarmac path before you reach gate, and follow it to the right, down through trees.

Brough Park

Go down Clerk Bank, on the right above the main road. At junction with Daisy Bank go straight on down cobbled path.

THE SWAN HOTEL

A523

ST EDWARDS ST.

CHURCH LANE

TOWN CENTRE

BANDSTAND

SAXON CROSSES

St Edward's Church

Market Place

Old Grammar Sch, Clerk Bank.

monks built back in the 13th century). It is hard to imagine today how this peaceful valley would have looked when the huge abbey church and cloisters stood just beyond Abbey Green, a settlement that grew up outside its gates. In common with all English monasteries, Dieulacres was dissolved by Henry VIII, in this case in 1538, and the church was sufficiently destroyed to prevent any immediate return to Catholic worship. Abbey Farm was built on the site in the early 1600s, by which time most of the buildings had been demolished and the stone sold and carted away. Today the few fragments that remain of this scheduled ancient monument are within the private farm, which incorporates a variety of pieces of monastic masonry.

⊠ **LEEK:** The town began to take shape around its market and association with the nearby abbey from the 13th century. The arrival of the canal and then the railway in the 19th century allowed the expansion primarily of the textile industry, and the town is fortunate that so many of the old stone and later brick structures from its past survive today. The walk leads you round the back of the old town along a new footpath from Abbey Green Road, with stunning views up the Churnet valley to the rocky outcrops of Hen Cloud and the Roaches (see Walk 14) before you turn into Brough Park. This was once the grounds of Ball Haye Hall, which stood roughly on the site of the sports centre, and was given to the town by the Brough family after the First World War. It opened as a public park in 1924 with the bandstand which you pass on your left erected in the same year. St Edward's church stands at the top of the park and is notable for the Saxon crosses that can be seen in its churchyard. Look also for the gravestone

of James Robinson near the base of the tower, who we are led to believe by the mason died at the ripe old age of 438! Look out on your left as you walk down Brow Hill for the imposing and appropriately named Big Mill. This impressive factory was built in 1857 by William Sugden, a local architect whose family was responsible for many notable Victorian buildings around the town.

Saxon cross, St Edward's church

REFRESHMENTS:

THE DYERS ARMS, Macclesfield Road, Leek. Open 12 noon to 11 pm every day. Telephone: 01538 382321.

THE HOTEL RUDYARD, Lake Road, Rudyard. Open 11 am to 11 pm (10.30 pm on Sunday). Telephone: 01538 306208.

THE ABBEY INN, Abbey Green, Leek. Open 11 am to 2 pm and 6.30 pm to 11 pm (closed on Tuesdays); all day opening on Saturday and Sunday in summer. Telephone: 01538 382865.

HARTINGTON

Length 2¾ miles

View of Hartington from Reynard's Lane

This is a short walk, which passes through three completely different landscapes in under three miles. The once thriving market town of Hartington is still resplendent in the trappings of its former status, with the imposing market hall and church tower dominating the stone cottages and Georgian houses that line the old market place. Yet only a short way on and you find yourself in the most luxurious of dales with the silky infant Dove gracefully stepping down a gorge surmounted by crags and glorious woodland. Once you drag yourself away from here it is an open country of lush green pasture cut up by stark white walls through which you return to Hartington, giving commanding views over the rooftops to the distant hills.

NB: Hartington gets very busy at weekends and through the holidays so plan to arrive early.

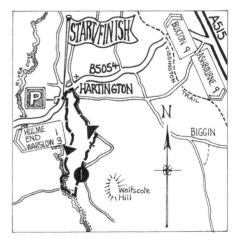

TERRAIN: One steady but short climb of just over 200 ft out of the dale. It can be wet alongside the river, even in summer.

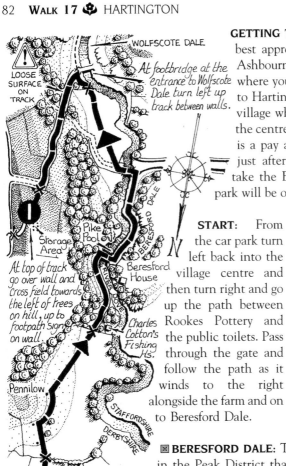

On the map:
WOLFSCOTE DALE
⚠ LOOSE SURFACE ON TRACK
At footbridge at the entrance to Wolfscote Dale turn left up track between walls.
Pike Pool
Storage Area
At top of track go over wall and cross field towards the left of trees on hill, up to footpath sign on wall.
Beresford House
Charles Cotton's Fishing Hs.
Pennilow
STAFFORDSHIRE
DERBYSHIRE
"Gap in wall"
Farm
B5054
Car Park
START/FINISH
Rookes Pottery
Toilets
HARTINGTON

GETTING THERE: From most directions the best approach is via the A515 Buxton to Ashbourne road just north of Newhaven where you turn onto the B5054, signposted to Hartington. After 2 miles you enter the village where you may find parking around the centre, but if you carry on through there is a pay and display car park on the right just after Rookes Pottery. From the west take the B5054 from Warslow and the car park will be on the left as you enter the village.

START: From the car park turn left back into the village centre and then turn right and go up the path between Rookes Pottery and the public toilets. Pass through the gate and follow the path as it winds to the right alongside the farm and on to Beresford Dale.

Beresford Dale

▨ **BERESFORD DALE:** There are few more beautiful spots in the Peak District than this richly wooded dale. It was named Beresford after an old crossing of the River Dove and a link with beavers (its earlier spelling was 'Beveresford'), but the Beresford family who took their name from the location preferred to use the more mighty bear on their coat of arms, which was implied by the later spelling! The dale has become famous for its fishing, as celebrated by Charles Cotton, who wrote the second part of Izaak Walton's *The Compleat Angler* in 1676. The old fishing house in which he and Walton spent much time still stands in the trees by the Dove (you can just see its pyramidal roof poking above the trees on your right as you approach the dale). Pike Pool (named after the pillar of limestone which stands at its edge, and not the fish) is one of the areas of water held back by the shallow weirs that were built to improve the river for fishing.

HARTINGTON

Garage
Pond
Old
Cheese Shop

The
Corner
House
Tea
Rooms

Village
Hall

St Giles
Church

CHARLES
COTTON
HOTEL

STONEWELL
LANE

Old
Town
Hall

Car
Park

Rookes
Pottery

Tea
Rooms

Old
Chapel

DEVONSHIRE
ARMS

Toilets

START FINISH

N

Farm

Turn left at
T junction and
follow lane back
to Hartington.

REYNARDS LANE

Pennilow

Staden
Barn

Pond

Barn

Pond

Go through gap
in wall just
past right
bend in road
and cross field
to gate and then
walk along lane.

Staden Barn

BERESFORD HALL: This old house stood on the Staffordshire bank of the Dove, high above the dale and was the home of Charles Cotton, who had inherited it through his mother Olive Stanhope, she being the granddaughter of Edward Beresford. Despite his fame, Cotton was always in debt and hid from his creditors in a cave in Beresford Dale, but by 1680 he had lost the estate and he died in London in 1687. The hall fared little better, slowly decaying until 1858 when it was mostly pulled down prior to a rebuilding, which never happened. A prospect tower (Beresford House) was rebuilt using material from the hall in 1905 and still stands above the cliffs on the west bank, while below and to the right is a cave, possibly the one used by Charles Cotton.

STADEN BARN AND REYNARD'S LANE: The landscape of limestone walls surrounding rich green pasture, which dominates the high ground in this area, was originally cut out of waste ground in the medieval period and divided into open strips for crops. Probably due to the poor soils these open fields were fairly quickly abandoned and divided up into the walled enclosures you see today, sometime before 1614 when they appear on an estate map.

HARTINGTON: The granting of a charter to hold a weekly market here in 1203 allowed Hartington to develop into a thriving local town complete with its 13th century church and a slightly later Perpendicular tower, standing on the

Hartington

high ground above the rooftops. Most of the buildings you see today are 18th and 19th century, many with limestone walls and gritstone quoins (corner stones) showing how close the town is to the border of these two geological areas. The old market place stands in the centre and is dominated by the imposing classical Market Hall of 1836 with its distinctive three arched openings at ground level (see picture). Around the corner, the duck pond is in another attractive setting; although of some age this is not ancient as it does not appear on the 1614 estate map. Overlooking this is the Old Cheese Shop, which highlights the importance of this product within the town. A factory for its production was established down Stonewell Lane shortly after 1870, but by 1894 it had been abandoned. Due to an outbreak of Foot and Mouth Disease in Leicestershire, a Stil-

ton producer from Melton Mowbray took over the site in 1900 and it is still in business today, making around 20% of the country's Stilton.

REFRESHMENTS:
THE CHARLES COTTON HOTEL, Hartington. Open 11 am to 11 pm (12 noon to 10.30 pm on Sunday). Telephone: 01298 84229.
THE DEVONSHIRE ARMS, Hartington. Summer opening: 11 am to 11 pm (12 noon to 10.30 pm on Sunday). Rest of the year: 11.30 am to 3 pm and 6 pm to 11 pm (12 noon to 3 pm and 7 pm to 11 pm on Sunday). Telephone: 01298 84232:
BERESFORD TEA ROOMS, Hartington. Open 10.30 am to 5 pm in summer and 10.30 am to 3 pm in winter. Telephone: 01298 84418.
CORNER HOUSE TEA ROOMS, Hartington. Open Saturday to Wednesday, 11 am to 5 pm in summer; Saturday and Sunday only in winter, 11 am to 4 pm. Telephone: 01298 84365.

Walk 18
GRINDON AND WETTON MILL
Length 3¼ miles

All Saints' Church, Grindon

The pastoral scene of gently rolling fields and scattered farmsteads which decorates this remote area of limestone plateau is seemingly held together by the spire of All Saints' church, a beacon for the traveller approaching the village of Grindon. This tranquillity, however, contrasts with the drama along the River Manifold only a stone's throw away. Towering rocky outcrops, huge gaping caves, deep wooded valleys and sheer limestone cliffs take the breath away at every turn. This is a walk that encompasses these two faces of the White Peaks, the untouched farming villages upon the high plateau and the spectacular river valleys below.

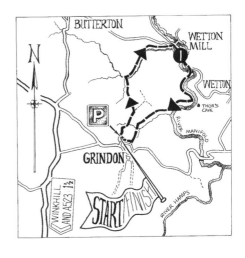

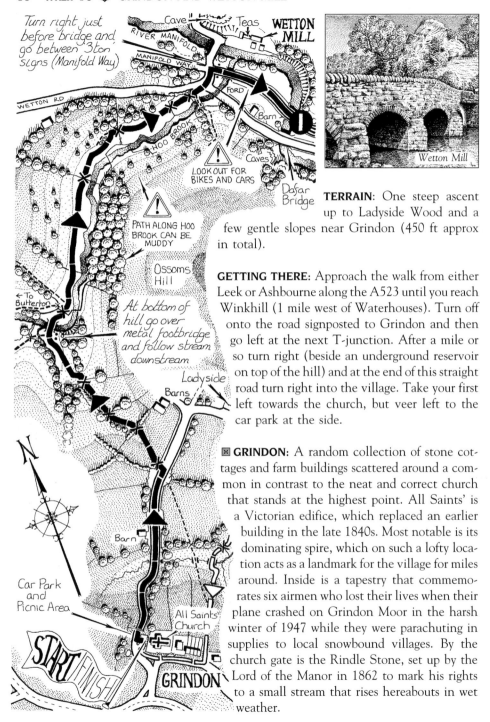

Turn right just before bridge and go between 3 ton signs (Manifold Way)

WETTON MILL

Cave Teas

RIVER MANIFOLD

MANIFOLD WAY

FORD

Barn

WETTON RD

HOO BROOK

Caves

Wetton Mill

LOOK OUT FOR BIKES AND CARS

Dafar Bridge

⚠ PATH ALONG HOO BROOK CAN BE MUDDY

Ossoms Hill

← To Butterton

At bottom of hill go over metal footbridge and follow stream downstream

Ladyside

Barns

N

Barn

Car Park and Picnic Area

All Saints' Church

START FINISH

GRINDON

TERRAIN: One steep ascent up to Ladyside Wood and a few gentle slopes near Grindon (450 ft approx in total).

GETTING THERE: Approach the walk from either Leek or Ashbourne along the A523 until you reach Winkhill (1 mile west of Waterhouses). Turn off onto the road signposted to Grindon and then go left at the next T-junction. After a mile or so turn right (beside an underground reservoir on top of the hill) and at the end of this straight road turn right into the village. Take your first left towards the church, but veer left to the car park at the side.

▨ **GRINDON:** A random collection of stone cottages and farm buildings scattered around a common in contrast to the neat and correct church that stands at the highest point. All Saints' is a Victorian edifice, which replaced an earlier building in the late 1840s. Most notable is its dominating spire, which on such a lofty location acts as a landmark for the village for miles around. Inside is a tapestry that commemorates six airmen who lost their lives when their plane crashed on Grindon Moor in the harsh winter of 1947 while they were parachuting in supplies to local snowbound villages. By the church gate is the Rindle Stone, set up by the Lord of the Manor in 1862 to mark his rights to a small stream that rises hereabouts in wet weather.

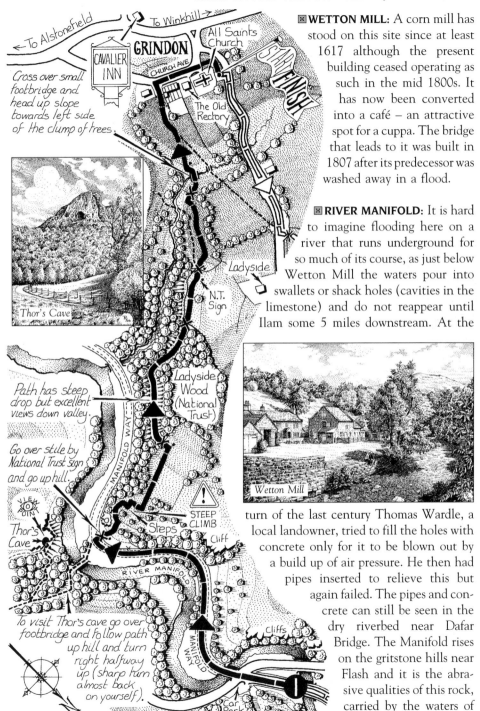

To Alstonefield

To Winkhill →

CAVALIER INN

GRINDON

All Saints Church

CHURCH AVE

The Old Rectory

SHAW FENCH

Cross over small footbridge and head up slope towards left side of the clump of trees.

Thor's Cave

Ladyside

N.T. Sign

Path has steep drop but excellent views down valley.

Ladyside Wood (National Trust)

MANIFOLD WAY

Go over stile by National Trust Sign and go up hill.

VIEW POINT

Thor's Cave

STEEP Steps CLIMB

⚠

Cliff

RIVER MANIFOLD

To visit Thor's Cave go over footbridge and follow path up hill and turn right halfway up (sharp turn almost back on yourself).

MANIFOLD WAY

Cliffs

Wetton Mill

Car Park

WETTON MILL: A corn mill has stood on this site since at least 1617 although the present building ceased operating as such in the mid 1800s. It has now been converted into a café – an attractive spot for a cuppa. The bridge that leads to it was built in 1807 after its predecessor was washed away in a flood.

RIVER MANIFOLD: It is hard to imagine flooding here on a river that runs underground for so much of its course, as just below Wetton Mill the waters pour into swallets or shack holes (cavities in the limestone) and do not reappear until Ilam some 5 miles downstream. At the turn of the last century Thomas Wardle, a local landowner, tried to fill the holes with concrete only for it to be blown out by a build up of air pressure. He then had pipes inserted to relieve this but again failed. The pipes and concrete can still be seen in the dry riverbed near Dafar Bridge. The Manifold rises on the gritstone hills near Flash and it is the abrasive qualities of this rock, carried by the waters of the river, that have created the steep gorges in the softer limestone of the White Peaks.

❋ **MINING:** Lead and copper have been mined in this area for centuries as a record of 1376 shows when a local vicar was arrested for his part in a theft of lead near Grindon! Many old shafts stand testimony to this trade, which peaked hereabouts in the late 18th century, and one is under the car park just to the north of Wetton Mill.

❋ **THE LEEK AND MANIFOLD VALLEY LIGHT RAILWAY:** Light railways are those which carry light traffic at low speeds and hence can be built more cheaply. The Light Railways Act of 1896 permitted further compromise on standards, which lowered construction costs again. This made lines built into areas like the Manifold valley profitable (well at least in theory!) so it was with much optimism that this narrow gauge railway from Waterhouses up along the river to Hulme End was opened in 1904. The money never poured in, though,

REFRESHMENTS:
THE CAVALIER, Grindon. Limited opening hours: 12 noon to 2.30 pm and 7 pm to 11 pm on Saturday and Sunday only. Telephone: 01538 304285. THE OLDE ROYAL OAK, Wetton. Open 12 noon to 3 pm and 7 pm to 11 pm (closed on Wednesdays in winter). Follow signs for Wetton from Grindon. Telephone: 01335 310287.
THE GEORGE INN, Waterhouses. On the A523 at the west end of the village. Telephone: 01538 308804.

and with the closure of a creamery at Ecton and competition from road traffic the railway was shut in 1934. Fortunately it was made into a footpath almost immediately and the route you take along the river is over the track bed and bridges of this line.

❋ **THOR'S CAVE:** This cavernous opening was probably formed by the river when the valley bottom was much higher. Relics of human occupation up until Roman times have been found here though today it is only a fiddle-playing ghost called Hobhurst who is said to reside here!

View of Manifold Valley from Thor's Cave

BRASSINGTON

Length 2½ miles

St James's Church, Brassington

The dramatic countryside that draws so many visitors to the Peak District does not stop abruptly at its boundary, as this rustic stone village surrounded by a landscape of rolling green fields and limestone cliffs demonstrates. Brassington is one of those Derbyshire villages that not only has the grandeur of a once important place but also a sleepy and quaint persona as if the modern world has passed it by. Its mix of mighty and humble stone buildings is further enhanced by their position on terraces along the slope of the hill. This short walk wanders through Brassington's back lanes and over to the dramatic tree-clad outcrops of limestone, which rise from fields littered with the remains of ancient farming and mining.

TERRAIN: Much of the route is on tarmac. There are a few gentle climbs.

NB: The footpath that leads up to Rainster Rocks is now overgrown. If you choose to scramble up here, you will have to veer round to the right halfway up and walk

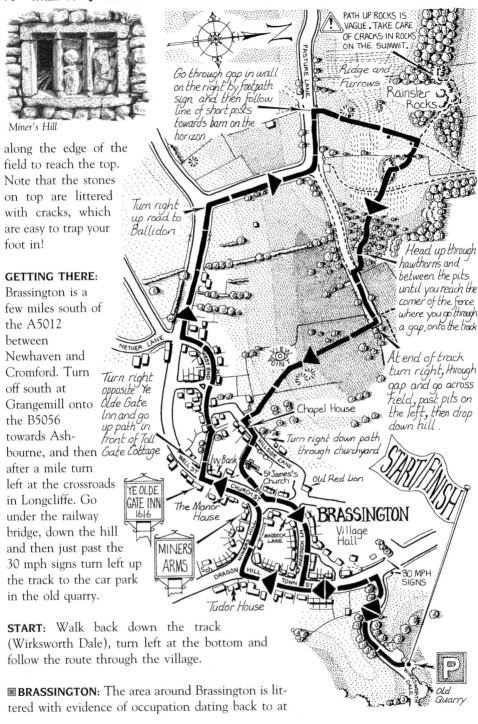

Miner's Hill

along the edge of the field to reach the top. Note that the stones on top are littered with cracks, which are easy to trap your foot in!

GETTING THERE:
Brassington is a few miles south of the A5012 between Newhaven and Cromford. Turn off south at Grangemill onto the B5056 towards Ashbourne, and then after a mile turn left at the crossroads in Longcliffe. Go under the railway bridge, down the hill and then just past the 30 mph signs turn left up the track to the car park in the old quarry.

START: Walk back down the track (Wirksworth Dale), turn left at the bottom and follow the route through the village.

⊞ **BRASSINGTON:** The area around Brassington is littered with evidence of occupation dating back to at

Text within the map:

PATH UP ROCKS IS VAGUE. TAKE CARE OF CRACKS IN ROCKS ON THE SUMMIT.

Go through gap in wall on the right by footpath sign and then follow line of short posts towards barn on the horizon

Ridge and Furrows

Rainster Rocks

Turn right up road to Ballidon

Head up through hawthorns and between the pits until you reach the corner of the fence where you go through a gap, onto the track

At end of track turn right, through gap and go across field, past pits on the left, then drop down hill.

NETHER LANE

Turn right opposite Ye Olde Gate Inn and go up path in front of Toll Gate Cottage

EAST END

VIEW POINT

Chapel House

Turn right down path through churchyard

Ivy Bank

WELL ST

HILLSIDE LANE

St James's Church

Old Red Lion

START/FINISH

YE OLDE GATE INN 1616

CHURCH ST

The Manor House

MINERS ARMS

MINERS HILL

MADDOCK LAKE

MADDOCK LN

BRASSINGTON

Village Hall

Sch

DRAGON HILL

TOWN ST

30 MPH SIGNS

Tudor House

P

WIRKSWORTH DALE

Old Quarry

View to Rainster Rocks

closed and the main road traffic ran else-where, so Brassington fell back into a slumber from which it has thankfully not awoken.

☒ **RAINSTER ROCKS:** This outcrop of dolomitised limestone (which has had magnesium introduced into its lime molecules to create this grey/brown craggy rock) has under its southern face a settlement dating from the Iron Age. There is further proof that man has worked the land here at a later date in the pits and heaps that litter the fields and the long strips of ridge and furrow that spread across them. The latter were formed by ploughing each side of a strip so that the spoil built up in the middle (it is not known if this was done on purpose to aid drainage).

least the Neolithic (New Stone Age) period, including settlements in the Iron Age and in Roman times around Rainster Rocks. The oldest part of the present village is the church, which dates back to the 12th century. Take a look inside and notice the simple circular piers and capitals with a rippling (scalloped) effect around the top, which date from this Norman period. While inside try and find an even earlier sculpture of a man holding his heart, somewhere on the inside of the west wall of the tower. The village you see today is dominated by fine 17th and 18th century houses, which were built when Brassington stood firstly on the old Derby to Manchester road and then the turnpike trust route dating from 1738 (Ye Olde Gate Inn and Tollhouse Cottage opposite record its presence). The Tudor House (1615) on Dragon Hill and The Manor House on Church Street (both private) are most impressive. The village's wealth, though, came from lead mining and the grassed over remains of the old shafts and spoil heaps still litter the countryside mainly to the east around the car park. But by the 19th century most of the mines were

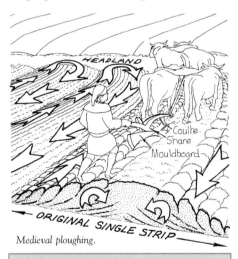

Medieval ploughing.

REFRESHMENTS:

THE MINERS ARMS, Brassington. Open 12 noon to 3 pm and 5.30 pm to 11 pm on weekdays; 11 am to 11 pm on Saturday; 12 noon to 10.30 pm on Sunday. Telephone: 01629 540222.

YE OLDE GATE INN, Brassington. Open 12 noon to 2.30 pm (3 pm on Saturday and Sunday) and 6 pm to 11 pm (10.30 pm on Sunday). No food on Mondays. Telephone: 01629 540448.

Walk 20
ILAM AND DOVEDALE
Length 5½ miles

Ilam

*F*ew places in the Peaks can compete with Dovedale for drama and Ilam for the picturesque. The deeply wooded ravine cut by the River Dove, with its limestone sentinels, majestic caves and cliffs seemingly scoured into grooves by a huge claw, contrasts with the pastoral scene above. Here gentle rolling fields of lime green grass divided up by stunning white stone walls sweep down to the idyllic collection of chocolate box cottages, rustic church and imposing grand hall of the ancient village of Ilam. Yet not all that we admire is as old as first it appears – as you will discover when you walk through this stunning landscape accompanied by the twittering of invisible birds overhead and the musical moods of the waters below.

NB: Ilam is very busy at weekends and bank holidays – arrive as early as possible.

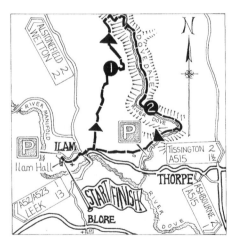

TERRAIN: One steep climb of approx 400 ft. The paths through the woods can be muddy in all seasons.

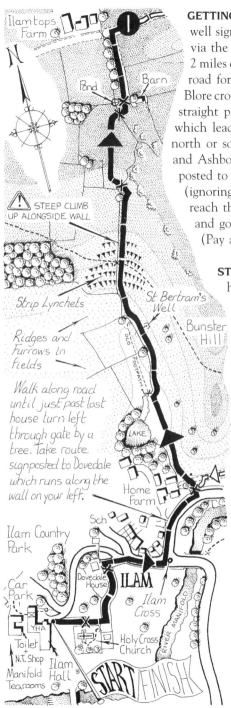

GETTING THERE: Ilam and Dovedale are generally well signposted. The best approach from the west is via the junction of the A52 and the A523 (approx 2 miles east of Waterhouses) where you take the Ilam road for about a mile and a half, then turn left at Blore crossroads. Follow the road down over the bridge, straight past the cross and through the gates ahead, which lead to the National Trust car park. From the north or south use the A515 and between Tissington and Ashbourne turn off onto the roads that are signposted to Ilam and Dovedale. After a couple of miles (ignoring the right turn to the Dovedale car park) you reach the village, where you turn right at the cross and go through the gates ahead into the car park (Pay and Display).

START: From the car park at the rear of the hall follow the 'Visitors' sign round the back of the building (where there are toilets, a shop and tearooms) and then pass under the main arch, which leads to the front (by the entrance to the Youth Hostel). Carry straight on to the path that runs along the left hand side of the church.

⌗ ST BERTRAM'S WELL: St Bertram was a Saxon noble who while studying in Ireland met and married a beautiful princess. While they were returning to England his wife gave birth in the forests of Wales, so Bertram briefly left her and the baby while he sought help. To his horror when he came back he found they had both been

An Ilam cottage

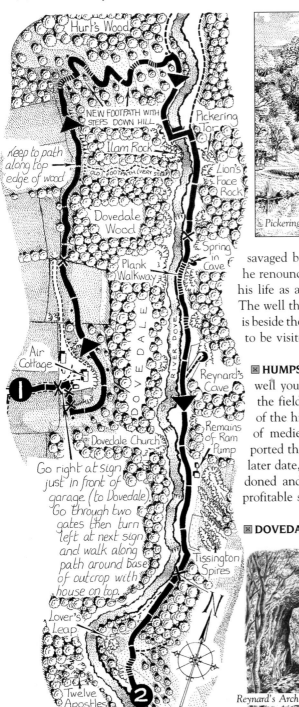

Labels on map:
Hurt's Wood
NEW FOOTPATH WITH STEPS DOWN HILL
Pickering Tor
Keep to path along top edge of wood
Ilam Rock
OLD FOOTPATH (VERY STEEP)
Lion's Face Rock
Dovedale Wood
Spring in Cave
Plank Walkway
33
Air Cottage
DOVEDALE
RIVER DOVE
Reynard's Cave
Remains of Ram Pump
Dovedale Church
Go right at sign just in front of garage (to Dovedale). Go through two gates then turn left at next sign and walk along path around base of outcrop with house on top.
Tissington Spires
Lover's Leap
Twelve Apostles
N

Pickering Tor

savaged by wolves, and filled with remorse he renounced the world and spent the rest of his life as a hermit in the area around Ilam. The well that was named after this local saint is beside the footpath although it is more likely to be visited by sheep than pilgrims today!

⊠ **HUMPS AND BUMPS:** In the area of the well you will notice ridges and furrows in the fields and steps (lynchets) in the side of the hill you walk up. These are remains of medieval ploughing, which once supported the old village of Ilam until, at some later date, the tilling of the fields was abandoned and they were turned over to more profitable sheep.

⊠ **DOVEDALE:** This dramatic gorge has been cut rapidly in geological terms due to a combination of soft limestone bedrock and abrasive grits carried by the water. This has left the harder rock as tall pillars or cliffs and caves stranded up high on the

Reynard's Arch

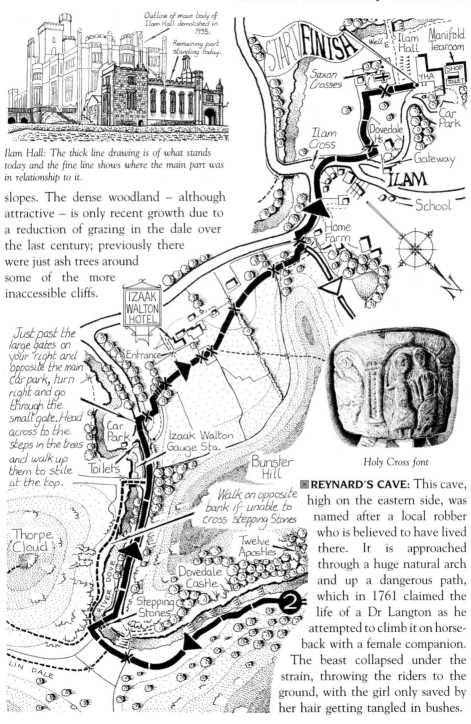

Ilam Hall: The thick line drawing is of what stands today and the fine line shows where the main part was in relationship to it.

slopes. The dense woodland – although attractive – is only recent growth due to a reduction of grazing in the dale over the last century; previously there were just ash trees around some of the more inaccessible cliffs.

Just past the large gates on your right and opposite the main car park, turn right and go through the small gate. Head across to the steps in the trees and walk up them to stile at the top.

Holy Cross font

⊠ **REYNARD'S CAVE:** This cave, high on the eastern side, was named after a local robber who is believed to have lived there. It is approached through a huge natural arch and up a dangerous path, which in 1761 claimed the life of a Dr Langton as he attempted to climb it on horseback with a female companion. The beast collapsed under the strain, throwing the riders to the ground, with the girl only saved by her hair getting tangled in bushes.

❈ **ILAM:** The village you see today was mainly rebuilt by Jesse Watts-Russell from the 1820s to the 1870s. He had made his fortune in industry and set about re-styling his wife's family estate. He removed the old medieval village, which had stood uncomfortably close to the hall, and built the attractive stone and tiled cottages at the present day site, with a new three-arched bridge next to the decorative cross that he had erected in memory of his first wife in 1840. From 1821–26 he encased the old hall within a huge Gothic styled mansion designed by Trubshaw, who had also worked on the nearby Alton Towers. The old medieval church was the only building from the original village to stay put, and Watts-Russell had a new octagonal chapel constructed on the north side in 1831 to house a memorial to his father-in-law, and then had Sir George Gilbert Scott give it a typically harsh make over. This idyllic Victorian estate was not to last, though, as the oversized hall was demolished in 1934–35 after an ill-fated venture as a restaurant,

with only the small section that survives today being saved by Robert MacDougal along with the estate, which he passed onto the National Trust. The hall is now a Youth Hostel and closed to other visitors but the old stable block at the back houses a shop and Discovery Centre. Holy Cross church is worth a visit, containing the base of St Bertram's medieval shrine and a rare 11th century font decorated with crude and fascinating figures. In the churchyard are the remains of two Saxon crosses, carved some 800 years before their more famous neighbour in the village.

REFRESHMENTS:

THE IZAAK WALTON HOTEL, Dovedale. A hotel in a beautiful setting, with a bar and restaurant that welcome walkers. Open 11 am to 3 pm and 6 pm to 11 pm (12 noon to 3 pm on Sunday). Telephone: 01335 350555.

NATIONAL TRUST TEA ROOMS, Ilam Hall. Open Saturday and Sunday throughout the year and Monday, Tuesday and Friday from mid May to the end of October, 11 am to 5 pm (4 pm in winter).

Thorpe Cloud